FOOD SAFETY

Other Books in the At Issue Series:

FOOD SAFETY

Laura K. Egendorf, *Book Editor*

David L. Bender, *Publisher*
Bruno Leone, *Executive Editor*

Bonnie Szumski, *Editorial Director*
David M. Haugen, *Managing Editor*

An Opposing Viewpoints® Series

Greenhaven Press, Inc.
San Diego, California

Library of Congress Cataloging-in-Publication Data

Food safety / Laura K. Egendorf, book editor.
      p.   cm. — (At issue)
   Includes bibliographical references and index.
   ISBN 0-7377-0151-X (lib. bdg. : alk. paper). —
ISBN 0-7377-0150-1 (pbk. : alk. paper)
   1. Food adulteration and inspection. 2. Food contamination.
I. Egendorf, Laura K., 1973– . II. Series: At issue (San Diego, Calif.)
TX531.F5677   2000
363.19'2—dc21   99-36429
                                                             CIP

Table of Contents

Introduction

For as long as there have been food safety laws, there have been people arguing that those laws have been overly stringent and based on nonexistent or overstated food scares. An early example of this was the public response to *The Jungle*, Upton Sinclair's 1906 novel that depicted working-class life in early twentieth-century Chicago. The book is best remembered for its description of the unsafe and horrific conditions at a canning factory, such as the use of diseased cows in canned meats and tales of men falling into vats and being processed into lard. The public outrage to the practices detailed in *The Jungle* led to the passage of the 1906 Federal Meat Inspection Act, which established sanitary standards for the meat industry and required the inspection of animals before and after slaughter. However, some critics have questioned whether the fear generated by *The Jungle* was justified, noting that Sinclair did not intend his book to be a wholly accurate portrayal of the Chicago meatpacking industry. As Sinclair himself explained, his intention was to gain sympathy for the working class, not to expose the meatpacking companies. "I aimed at the public's heart, and by accident I hit it in the stomach," he said. According to a 1998 article by Professor E.C. Pasour, "[Sinclair] did not even pretend to have actually witnessed or verified the horrendous conditions he ascribed to Chicago packing houses. . . . Indeed, a congressional investigation at the time found little substance in Sinclair's allegations."

Ninety years after *The Jungle* appeared in print, another threat to meat safety was widely publicized. The "mad cow" epidemic raises a question similar to that inspired by Sinclair's book—whether the meat supply is unsafe and steps should be taken by the government to improve the practices of the meat industry, or whether the public is too easily frightened by media hype.

A look at mad cow disease

Mad cow disease is formally known as bovine spongiform encephalopathy (BSE). Spongiform encephalopathies are diseases that gradually destroy the brain and central nervous system; the victims' brain tissue appears sponge-like when examined under a microscope. The first outbreaks of mad cow disease occurred in Britain in the mid-1980s, the result of cows being fed sheep brains and spinal columns infected with scrapie, a rare sheep disease that got its name because affected sheep exhibit unusual itching behavior, eventually scraping away large portions of their wool. The sheep also weaken, have trouble walking, and typically die within a few months of catching the disease. Britain responded to the mad cow crisis by banning the use of animals in cattle feed and killing all cows that exhibited symptoms of BSE, which include aggressive and unpredictable behavior and difficulty standing and walking. The United

States also took action by banning the import of British cattle and meat products in 1989.

Mad cow disease garnered increased attention in 1995, when ten Britons died from a new strain of Creutzfeldt-Jakob disease (CJD), a human disease similar to mad cow. The following year, the British government announced that a link possibly existed between the new strain of CJD (nvCJD) and the consumption of BSE-infected meat. That theory gained credence in March 1999, when a report by the National Academy of Sciences in the District of Columbia stated that mad cow disease can be transmitted to primates through food. As of March 1999, thirty-nine people had died from nvCJD. The symptoms, similar to BSE and scrapie, include memory loss, depression, and a loss of balance. Victims become unable to care for themselves, slipping into comas or baby-like states before dying.

Although the total number of deaths from nvCJD has been small, and there have been no known cases of mad cow–related CJD disease in the United States as of June 1999, the public—especially in North America and Europe—has been largely frightened by the possibility the disease could reach epidemic proportions. In 1996, British microbiologist Dr. Richard Lacey predicted that up to 500,000 Britons could die each year from nvCJD. One reason why some people fear a catastrophic death rate is that CJD has an incubation period of ten to fifteen years. Thus, even people who have become vegetarians could remain at risk for the disease. One victim who may have developed the disease after a lengthy incubation was Peter Hall, who had stopped eating meat prior to exhibiting the symptoms in December 1994. He died fourteen months later at age twenty. Hall, like many of the other victims, was a healthy young adult; the more common strains of CJD afflicted older people. In addition to eating contaminated meat, some of the victims had worked with meat, either as teenagers or adults.

Public reaction

The mad cow scare led to widespread changes in eating habits. The worldwide beef industry lost $10 billion in 1996, due to a decrease in consumption and importation. Government officials in Britain removed beef from the menus of approximately two thousand schools. By May 1996, beef consumption had fallen by 25 percent in Britain and 30 percent in the European Union, while the United States decreased its import of cattle by 1 percent. Government and business policy in the United States also changed, as the Food and Drug Administration (FDA) banned the use of bone and meat meal in cattle and sheep feed in June 1996.

Although European consumption of cattle had begun to return to earlier levels by 1998, and the United States increased its beef imports by 10 percent in 1997, some people made more permanent changes. In an article for the *Atlantic Monthly*, Ellen Ruppel Shell explains how the BSE scare changed her family's shopping and cooking habits. "I avoid any ground meat that hasn't been ground in the store where I buy it. . . . And my eight-year-old daughter has forsaken lunch meats for what she calls 'vegetarian burgers,' which consist of a slice of American cheese melted over two sandwich pickles on a bun."

Part of the drop in meat industry profits and consumption was due to the influence of the media. Just as it had in 1906, when *The Jungle* was published, the American public reacted strongly to news about unsafe practices at farms and processing plants. In 1906, a book had played a key role. Nine decades later, a television program proved to be particularly influential. In April 1996, television talk show host Oprah Winfrey aired an interview with former rancher Howard Lyman, who claimed that the practice of feeding ground-up animal parts to cattle could lead to a mad cow epidemic in the United States. Upon hearing this, Winfrey stated that she would never eat another hamburger. Following the show's broadcast, the demand for beef fell—cattle prices decreased 10 percent over the next two weeks, costing cattlemen millions of dollars. A group of Texas cattlemen sued Oprah over their loss in profits, arguing that she had created an unnecessary panic. The lawsuit stated in part: "The carefully and maliciously edited statements [on the show] were designed to hype the ratings at the expense of the American cattle industry. . . . The statements disparaged the safety of American beef, and intentionally placed unfounded and unwarranted fear in the beef consumer's mind." Winfrey won the suit in February 1998 but the verdict was appealed. As of June 1999, the appellate court had not reached a decision. Cattle rancher Paul Engler, one of the plaintiffs in the first suit, filed a second suit against Winfrey; as of this writing, a decision had not been reached.

The Texas cattlemen were not the only group who questioned the public's reaction to mad cow disease. Many media commentators have also contended that the threat has been overhyped. In an article in the March 30, 1996, issue of *The Spectator*, a British weekly, Frank Johnson questions the popular response to the scientific reports on BSE, reports he considers misleading. "The scientists spoke, and the result was hysteria from interviewers, tabloids and liberal broadsheets. Yet the people whipping it up did not believe it."

Meat-related deaths in the United States

While nvCJD has yet to kill Americans, other types of meat contamination have proved fatal. In late 1992 and early 1993, four children died and hundreds of people became sick after eating undercooked hamburgers at Jack in the Box. Those burgers contained the *Escherichia coli* (*E. coli*) O157:H7 bacteria, which can only be killed if the meat is cooked thoroughly. In addition, twenty-one people died and 100 more became ill in 1998 after eating Sara Lee hot dogs and cold cuts that harbored the listeria microbe. Other dangerous bacteria include salmonella, which is found in raw meat, seafood, poultry and eggs, as well as animal feces, and can cause up to 3,800 deaths each year.

As with the 1906 meat inspection act and the 1989 and 1996 bans on cattle and certain feeds, the government has responded to these dangers by imposing new regulations and warnings. In 1995, a food-safety system called Hazard Analysis and Critical Control Points (HACCP) was implemented to test the safety of seafood; its use was expanded in 1996 to meat and poultry. Under the HACCP system, slaughterhouse and plant managers identify points in the production process where contamination could occur and take steps to prevent that contamination. The listeria outbreak led to a May 1999 U.S. Department of Agriculture warning that advised pregnant women, the elderly, and small children to avoid eating soft cheeses and processed meats, unless the meat is reheated until steaming hot. However, as health care writer Sue Carls points out in an article in *The World & I,* the public should not assume that these regulations will guarantee a safe food supply. According to Carls, "Many of the cases of foodborne bacteria begin well outside the processing plant. The mishandling of food at the consumer level is a huge factor."

Whether nvCJD will become epidemic remains to be seen. Although that particular threat to food safety may turn out to be overhyped, contaminants in the U.S. food supply have led to illnesses that are estimated to kill more than nine thousand Americans each year and sicken millions more. Consequently, the food safety debate extends beyond the actual risks of certain foods and into the question of what steps, if any, need to be taken to ensure the improved and continued safety of the American food supply. In *Food Safety: At Issue,* the authors consider the causes of food-borne illnesses and evaluate possible solutions.

1

America's Food Supply Is Safe

National Cattlemen's Beef Association

The National Cattlemen's Beef Association (NCBA) is a trade associa-
tion, marketing organization, and advocate for America's cattle farmers
and ranchers. Its members work to ensure the safety and quality of
American beef.

The food supply in America, especially its beef supply, is safe.
When food-borne illnesses occur, the cause is more likely the improper handling or preparation of food, instead of the use of
chemicals and pesticides by farmers and ranchers. The efforts of
the federal government and the beef industry help ensure that
America's food does not pose health risks.

A mericans have the safest food supply in the world. No other country
can match the effective food safety record of the United States—no
other country monitors domestically-produced and imported foods as
closely.

No responsible scientist in the food system would deny there are substances
in the food supply that could be nasty if consumed in excess amounts, but bod-
ies aren't piling up because of lethal substances in food. Diet-related health con-
ditions are related to our overall habits, not to specific food chemicals, present
in minuscule amounts.—Dr. Joyce Nettleton, Institute of Food Technolo-
gists, 1996.

From my 22 years in researching and studying food and food safety, I have
total confidence in the safety of the U.S. food supply. Can foods be safer? Yes.
And the food industry and government are working diligently on new technolo-
gies and programs to improve the safety and quality of foods.—Dr. H. Russell
Cross, professor of animal science at Texas A&M University and former
administrator of the U.S. Agriculture Department's (USDA) Food Safety
and Inspection Service (FSIS), *Dallas Morning News,* May 27, 1994.

Our society has come to fear technology and reject anything scientifically or
chemically related. Despite all the evidence of our physical well-being beyond
the dreams of all previous generations, we seem to have become a nation of eas-

Reprinted from National Cattlemen's Beef Association pamphlet, *Cattle and Beef Handbook,*
October 1997, available at http://www.beef.org/librref/beefhand/food1.html.

ily frightened people. Americans have been described as "the healthiest hypochondriacs in the world."—Dr. James Marsden, vice president, Scientific and Technical Affairs, American Meat Institute, "A Scientist's Perspective on Food Safety," *Nation's Restaurant News*, Aug. 27, 1990.

The U.S. beef supply is safe

- There are no "hidden ingredients" in fresh cuts of beef.
- Fresh cuts of beef are not treated with additives or preservatives.
- Used judiciously, animal-health products and other compounds currently used in cattle production and feeding do not cause residue problems.

A major reason overseas customers purchase U.S. beef is confidence in its safety. . . . U.S. government monitoring and inspection programs are recognized around the world, as is the cattle industry's Beef Quality Assurance Program which helps prevent hazardous residue.—Dr. Gary Smith, meat scientist, Colorado State University, 1995.

As shown by government residue testing and monitoring, American cattlemen continue to produce beef without hazardous residues.—Dr. Gary Cowman, National Cattlemen's Beef Association (NCBA) director of Beef Quality Assurance, 1996.

The progress we've made in the last decade shows that meat and poultry products are safe from chemical contaminants. Our testing data give convincing evidence, and the new preventive approach holds great promise for the future. We are confident that chemical residues in meat and poultry pose little risk to consumers.—Dr. Catherine E. Adams, FSIS, USDA, 1990.

Risk assessors rank the health risks from chemical residues in food products as negligible because residues are generally so small that they are unlikely to threaten even the most susceptible and most exposed individuals with a significant risk of cancer or other diseases.—USDA, 1995.

Consumers have more confidence in the safety of beef than any other meat. Even though beef attracts media scrutiny because more of it is consumed on a daily basis than other meats, consumers consistently give beef high marks for safety.

Chemicals and pesticides are not harmful

A small segment of the industry's producers and purveyors has built niche markets for a product that carries the USDA natural label. While this product may be the result of cattle that have not been treated with antibiotics or implanted with hormones, in reality, all fresh beef qualifies for the natural label. By law, natural products must contain no food additives and be minimally processed. Test results from Colorado State University in 1995 conclude beef raised from cattle raised without the use of growth promotants or other technological tools was not significantly different from traditionally produced beef.

Fresh Beef Is Very Low in Illness-Causing Bacteria. Salmonella organisms are found less often on beef than other meats. According to USDA, based on sampling at processing plants, fresh beef is very low in incidence of Salmonella on the meat; 35.2 percent of chicken broiler samples contained Salmonella; 12 percent of pork samples contained Salmonella organisms; and only 1.8 percent of beef samples contained Salmonella.

Foodborne illness is caused primarily by improper storage, handling and preparation of foods.

Consumers can be assured that FSIS is testing the U.S. meat and poultry supply for drug and chemical contaminants. Any problems are dealt with quickly. Where consumers can be most effective is in controlling conditions in their own kitchens that might allow growth of bacteria that can lead to illness.—Dr. Richard Carnevale, FSIS, 1991.

The U.S. Department of Agriculture estimates that a quarter of the estimated 8 million cases of food-borne illness each year could have been prevented by safe food practices.—Dr. Robert Gravani, *Food Technology* magazine, February 1992.

Chemical residues in food are not a problem. The government system of approval for animal drugs and pesticides builds in sweeping safety margins. As an example, maximum levels of pesticide residue allowed in or on food are 100–1,000 times lower than could pose a threat over a lifetime. The Agriculture Council of America says a 150 lb. adult would have to eat 3,000 heads of lettuce each day for the rest of his/her life to ingest an amount of pesticide found to cause problems in laboratory mice.

Americans have the safest food supply in the world.

Possible chemical contamination of our food supply is not a serious threat. Regulation of food additives, pesticides and animal drugs helps assure ample protection of the public. There is no evidence that pesticides in our foods constitute a significant health hazard.—Dr. Michael W. Pariza, director, Food Research Institute, chairman, Department of Food Microbiology and Toxicology, University of Wisconsin, December 1991.

Naturally occurring compounds in food pose a far greater risk than synthetic ones—and that risk is negligible.

Ordinary table spices, including mustard and peppers, contain a variety of naturally occurring carcinogens which pose substantially higher risks than do any pesticide residues or food additives. If we want to reduce the risk of death by cancer, we have to look first at the naturally occurring carcinogens found in foods. Cancer is an important public health concern, but if we attack it by chasing after specific ingredients such as Alar or Red Dye 3, we're not going to make much of a difference. That is because food additives, as well as animal-health products, have been thoroughly tested before being implemented.—Dr. Robert Scheuplein, director, Toxicological Sciences, Center for Food Safety and Applied Nutrition, Food and Drug Administration, 1991.

All animal drugs and pesticides used on crops fed to livestock go through rigorous testing before approval by the FDA or EPA.

The FDA either sets zero tolerance for drug residues or it sets tolerances based on extensive research and testing. It's important to keep in mind that we build a 1,000-fold or 2,000-fold safety factor (for allergic reactions) into our tolerances (for animal drug residues). This helps to avoid ill effects even when a residue occurs that slightly exceeds the legal limit. The same (principle) holds true for the potential risk of cancer from residues of carcinogenic drugs (in animal tests). We aren't aware of any cases of cancer than can be linked to drug residues in food.—Dr. Gerald Guest, FDA, 1989.

Violative residues in livestock and poultry continue to decline each year. They were lower in 1993 than 1992. Drug residues in beef continued to decline; of 5,439 samples of beef tested last year, eight had illegal levels of drugs and all eight violations occurred in cull dairy cows. There were no pesticide residue violations in the 5,439 beef samples.—Dr. Richard Carnevale, FSIS.

Bacteria and other micro-organisms in food are a more serious health issue than chemical residues. Although consumers express concern about chemical contamination, most experts believe microbial contamination poses a greater hazard to human health than pesticide or animal drug residues.—People, the Public Health & Consumer Protection, USDA FSIS, 1990.

BSE poses no threat to U.S. consumers. Bovine Spongiform Encephalopathy (BSE), inappropriately dubbed by some as Mad Cow Disease, is a degenerative neurological disease in cattle. It was first identified in England in 1986. An outbreak of the disease in England in 1995 caused world-wide concern when speculation arose that BSE might be linked to a rare brain condition in humans known as Creutzfeldt-Jakob Disease (CJD).

- USDA has tested thousands of cattle brains and never found BSE in the United States.
- Since 1989, the U.S. has banned imports of live ruminant animals and ruminant products from the United Kingdom and other countries where BSE has been identified.
- There is no scientific evidence that BSE in cattle and CJD in humans are linked.
- CJD occurs at a consistent rate of one case per million people per year among vegetarians and meat eaters alike, in countries where BSE has been found and has not been found.

. . . The evidence against British beef is purely circumstantial. And, since no cases of BSE have been identified in the U.S., there currently seems to be no reason in this country to worry about CJD from eating beef.—Susan Male Smith, M.A., R.D., cited in *Environmental Nutrition*, 1996.

BSE is not found in the muscle tissue of cattle eaten as beef. Scientific evidence indicates beef and milk do not present a risk to people as there is no evidence the agent that causes BSE is present in muscle and milk.—International Food Information Council, September 1996.

Government and market inspections

Federal inspection systems ensure consumer safety. More than 2 million analyses of meat and poultry samples are performed each year. USDA's Food Safety and Inspection Service obtains samples of tissue from harvested animals and analyzes those samples. Findings are sent to FDA field offices for follow-up. Regulatory action is taken against those responsible for any residues above legal limits.

Health experts agree food-safety problems stem mainly from improper storage and handling by those who prepare food rather than from residues in food.

There is no food product more closely scrutinized by the government before it is purchased by consumers than meat. USDA devotes eight times the resources to inspecting the nation's meat and poultry as the Food and Drug Administration devotes to the rest of the food supply. The federal government spends more than $1 million each day employing USDA's 7,000 meat and poultry inspectors *who are in every packing plant, every minute it operates, every day it operates. By comparison, FDA-inspected food plants may see their inspector once every several years.*—J. Patrick Boyle, president and CEO, American Meat Institute, January 1992.

Cattlemen go the extra mile with Beef Quality Assurance. To ensure continued safety and to maintain consumer confidence, the beef industry initiated a Beef Quality Assurance (BQA) program in 1987 that focuses on product safety. The Beef Quality Assurance program encourages cattlemen in every state to follow production practices and quality-control measures that exceed government requirements as related to pharmaceutical use. Besides cow/calf producers, a 1994 USDA survey showed almost 87 percent of the nation's feedlots had quality-assurance training for employees.

Foodborne illness is caused primarily by improper storage, handling and preparation of foods.

The program does not add cost to the final product. In fact, since the program began, it has saved the beef industry in excess of $20 million, helping the industry stabilize product cost to consumers.

Beef Quality Assurance is a way for cattlemen to prevent any possible hazardous residues and to demonstrate to consumers that the industry is committed to producing a safe and wholesome product.

The program promotes use of production practices and quality control for animal-pharmaceutical use that provide safety measures which exceed government requirements. The BQA program also teaches cattlemen and feedlot operators about cattle handling, feed purchasing, record keeping, testing and other procedures.

It is simply a way for cattlemen to prevent any possible hazardous residues and to demonstrate that cattlemen remain committed to producing a safe, nutritious, healthful product for consumers with no added ingredients or preservatives.

$1 billion a year—$4 per consumer—is spent on beef-safety programs by the packing industry to ensure that beef products are completely safe.

Government tests show there are no hazardous residue levels of any chemical compound in beef. In fact, U.S. Department of Agriculture (USDA) tests repeatedly demonstrate that beef, of all fresh food commodities, has one of the safest records for lack of chemical contamination.—Dr. Gary Cowman, Director of Beef Quality Assurance, National Cattlemen's Beef Association, September 1994.

New HACCP regulations aimed at improved safety. In 1996 USDA adopted the Hazard Analysis and Critical Control Points (HACCP) regulation which requires all meat and poultry processing plants to develop and implement HACCP programs. In a nutshell, HACCP is a systematic, comprehensive science-based approach to assure the production of safe food. The new regulation requires all processing plants to conduct regular microbial testing of raw meat to verify that process control for fecal contamination—the source of pathogens—is working.

For more than 10 years, the National Academy of Sciences, university researchers and beef producers and packers have urged that inspections be made more science-based, focusing on control of invisible bacteria and not just visually identified problems. With the new HACCP-based regulations, we can further improve beef safety. Beef already has a good microbiological profile. Now, with the further use of new technologies and modern procedures, we can do even more to remove any contaminants and destroy pathogenic bacteria. Meanwhile, of course, proper cooking and handling remain important too.—Dr. Gary Weber, NCBA director of animal health and meat inspection, *The Beef Brief,* August 1996.

Beef processors must meet zero-tolerance standards. Even though, poultry is allowed a defined number of defects before inspection action is taken, beef conforms to a zero-tolerance standard for fecal and ingesta contamination which required carcass trimming in the past. Aggressive industry efforts have resulted in new technology—such as high temperature vacuuming—which enables compliance with zero-tolerance standards while helping to eliminate carcass waste.

Beef cattle producers and companies have invested millions of dollars to develop HACCP plans and new technologies, such as the high temperature steam vacuum system, to ensure beef and beef products continue to be safe and wholesome. The implementation of HACCP in every plant will add an additional measure of safety to our products.—John Lacey, former NCBA president, 1996.

Understanding beef safety

Q. How does the safety of beef compare to that of other fresh meats?

A. Beef is one of the safest foods available to consumers. USDA and FDA tests indicate that, among all fresh commodities, beef has the lowest probability of contamination by either chemicals or microbes.

Q. Are there any pesticide or antibiotic residues in beef?

A. Substantial testing has shown that the violative residue rate (antibiotic, chemical and pesticide) is virtually zero in beef.

Q. Cattlemen appear to have some limits on their ability to prevent possible residues in beef. What about factors over which they do not have direct control? For example, using feeds they didn't grow which might contain potentially hazardous levels of pesticides?

A. First, there is no evidence that pesticides on crops are causing health problems as a result of beef use. Second, the industry's safety assurance program calls for testing of feed ingredients to assure that there are no violative levels of pesticides. Another factor is, no matter what kind of environmental contaminant or toxin (such as a natural or a man-made pesticide) might be in feed or water, animals generally eliminate the noxious substance by naturally biodegrading it.

Beef is one of the safest foods available to consumers.

Q. What is the responsibility of federal regulators and inspectors in helping assure safe products?

A. Federal regulators screen and approve new products and technologies, such as feed additives. It is possible that an isolated food grower, as well as a processor and marketer, will not adequately guard against chemical or microbial contamination, so both legal requirements and voluntary safety-assurance programs are advisable.

Q. Some activists claim "factory farming" and other techniques are poisoning the food supply. Is that true?

A. No. The food supply is the safest it has ever been in this country. Health experts in this country agree that safety problems associated with food are primarily due to improper storage and handling by food preparers and consumers, not because of residues found in the food.

Q. Are "naturally" or "organically" grown foods safer?

A. There is no evidence that "organically" raised beef is safer than "conventionally" raised beef. Results of 1992 and 1994 studies at Colorado State University revealed no violative residues in beef. There are 16,000 times more residues from "naturally" occurring pesticides in foods than residues from synthetic compounds. But in both cases, the food is safe.

2

Foodborne Illnesses Are on the Rise

Robert A. Robinson

Robert A. Robinson is the associate director of food and agriculture is-sues at the Resources, Community and Economic Development Division of the U.S. Department of Agriculture.

Contamination in the U.S. food supply has led to an increase in often-deadly food-borne illnesses. Possible causes for the growing risk include deadlier strains of bacteria such as *E. coli*, broader dis-tribution of contaminated foods, and improper handling and preparation. These illnesses kill over nine thousand people each year and sicken millions more. Although the government has worked to reduce food safety risks, fragmented responsibilities among various federal agencies have stymied those efforts.

Editor's Note: The following viewpoint was originally a statement given to the House of Representatives Subcommittee on Human Resources and Intergovern-mental Relations on May 23, 1996.

We are pleased to be here to participate in this hearing on foodborne pathogens and their impact on public health. In previous reports and testimonies, we have discussed many aspects of food safety, includ-ing inspection and coordination activities and efforts to protect against unsafe chemical residues and microbiological hazards. Today, as you re-quested, we will focus on what is and is not known about the scope, severity, and cost of foodborne illnesses in the United States. We will also summarize our prior work on the structural problems that limit the fed-eral government's ability to ensure food safety.

Government monitoring of food safety

In summary, in our May 1996 report on foodborne illnesses,[1] we reported that existing data, although incomplete, indicate that foodborne illnesses

Reprinted from Robert A. Robinson's statement given to the House of Representatives, Committee on Government Reform and Oversight, Subcommittee on Human Resources and Intergovern-mental Relations, May 23, 1996.

are widespread and costly. Specifically, the best available data on food-borne illnesses demonstrate the following:

• Millions of illnesses and thousands of deaths in the United States each year can be traced to contaminated food. Moreover, the actual incidence may be much higher because public health experts believe that most cases are not reported. These experts also believe that the risk of foodborne illnesses has been increasing over the last 20 years.

• Foodborne illnesses generally cause temporary disorders of the digestive tract, but they can also lead to serious, long-term health consequences. Recent estimates of the cost of foodborne illnesses range from over $5 billion to over $22 billion annually. For example, the cost of medical treatment and lost productivity related to foodborne illnesses from seven of the most harmful bacteria ranged from $5.6 billion to $9.4 billion in 1993.

While providing useful indicators concerning the extent of foodborne illnesses, existing data have limitations. Public health and food safety experts believe that current data on foodborne illnesses do not provide a complete picture of the risk level and do not depict the sources of contamination and the populations most at risk in sufficient detail. More uniform and comprehensive data on the number and causes of foodborne illnesses could enable the development of more effective control strategies. While federal and state agencies have begun to collect such data in five areas across the country, federal officials expressed some concern about whether they would be able to continue funding this discretionary effort.

Providing more comprehensive data would help federal food safety officials develop better control strategies but would not address the structural problems with the food safety system. As we have previously reported,[2] the system evolved over many years in response to specific health threats and new technological developments, resulting in a patchwork of inconsistent approaches that weaken its effectiveness. Food products with similar risks are subject to different rules, limited inspection resources are not efficiently used, and agencies must engage in extensive and often unsuccessful coordination activities in an attempt to address food safety activities.

Between 6.5 million and 81 million cases of foodborne illness and as many as 9,100 related deaths occur each year.

The Centers for Disease Control and Prevention (CDC) in the Department of Health and Human Services is the federal agency primarily responsible for monitoring the incidence of foodborne illness in the United States. In collaboration with state and local health departments and other federal agencies, CDC investigates outbreaks of foodborne illnesses and supports disease surveillance, research, prevention efforts, and training related to foodborne illnesses. CDC coordinates its activities concerning the safety of the food supply with the Food and Drug Administration (FDA), which is also in the Department of Health and Human Services. With respect to the safety of meat, poultry, and eggs, CDC coordinates with the Food Safety and Inspection Service (FSIS) in the U.S.

Department of Agriculture (USDA).

CDC monitors individual cases of illness from harmful bacteria, viruses, chemicals, and parasites (hereafter referred to collectively as pathogens) that are known to be transmitted by foods, as well as foodborne outbreaks, through voluntary reports from state and local health departments, FDA, and FSIS. In practice, because CDC does not have the authority to require states to report data on foodborne illnesses, each state determines which diseases it will report to CDC. In addition, state laboratories voluntarily report the number of positive test results for several diseases that CDC has chosen to monitor. However, these reports do not identify the source of infection and are not limited to cases of foodborne illness. CDC also investigates a limited number of more severe or unusual outbreaks when state authorities request assistance.

The causes and growth of foodborne illnesses

At least 30 pathogens are associated with foodborne illnesses. For reporting purposes, CDC categorizes the causes of outbreaks of foodborne illnesses as bacterial, chemical, viral, parasitic, or unknown pathogens. Although many people associate foodborne illnesses primarily with meat, poultry, eggs, and seafood products, many other foods—including milk, cheese, ice cream, orange and apple juices, cantaloupes, and vegetables—have also been involved in outbreaks during the last decade.

Bacterial pathogens are the most commonly identified cause of outbreaks of foodborne illnesses. Bacterial pathogens can be easily transmitted and can multiply rapidly in food, making them difficult to control. CDC has targeted four of them—*E. coli* O157:H7, *Salmonella* Enteritidis, *Listeria monocytogenes*, and *Campylobacter jejuni*—as being of greatest concern.

The existing data on foodborne illnesses have weaknesses and may not fully depict the extent of the problem. In particular, public health experts believe that the majority of cases of foodborne illness are not reported because the initial symptoms of most foodborne illnesses are not severe enough to warrant medical attention, the medical facility or state does not report such cases, or the illness is not recognized as foodborne. However, according to the best available estimates, based largely on CDC's data, millions of people become sick from contaminated food each year, and several thousand die. In addition, public health and food safety officials believe that the risk of foodborne illnesses is increasing for several reasons.

Between 6.5 million and 81 million cases of foodborne illness and as many as 9,100 related deaths occur each year, according to the estimates provided by several studies conducted since 1986. The wide range in the estimated number of foodborne illnesses and related deaths is due primarily to the considerable uncertainty about the number of cases that are never reported to CDC. For example, CDC officials believe that many intestinal illnesses that are commonly referred to as the stomach flu are caused by foodborne pathogens. People do not usually associate these illnesses with food because the onset of symptoms occurs 2 or more days after the contaminated food was eaten.

Furthermore, most physicians and health professionals treat patients who have diarrhea without ever identifying the specific cause of the illness. In severe or persistent cases, a laboratory test may be ordered to identify the responsible pathogen.

Finally, physicians may not associate the symptoms they observe with a pathogen that they are required to report to the state or local health authorities. For example, a CDC official cited a Nevada outbreak in which no illnesses from *E. coli* O157:H7 had been reported to health officials, despite a requirement that physicians report such cases to the state health department. Nevertheless, 58 illnesses from this outbreak were subsequently identified. In the absence of more complete reporting, researchers can only broadly estimate the number of illnesses and related deaths.

Food safety and public health officials believe that several factors are contributing to an increased risk of foodborne illnesses. First, the food supply is changing in ways that can promote foodborne illnesses. For example, as a result of modern animal husbandry techniques, such as crowding a large number of animals together, the pathogens that can cause foodborne illnesses in humans can spread throughout the herd. Also, because of broad distribution, contaminated food products can reach more people in more locations.

Subsequent mishandling can further compound the problem. For example, leaving perishable food at room temperature increases the likelihood of bacterial growth and undercooking reduces the likelihood that bacteria will be killed. Knowledgeable experts believe that although illnesses and deaths often result from improper handling and preparation, the pathogens were, in many cases, already present at the processing stage.

Second, because of demographic changes, more people are at greater risk of contracting a foodborne illness. In particular, certain populations are at greater risk for these illnesses: people with suppressed immune systems, children in group settings like daycare, and the elderly.

Third, three of the four pathogens CDC considers the most important were unrecognized as causes of foodborne illness 20 years ago—*Campylobacter*, *Listeria*, and *E. coli* O157:H7.

Fourth, bacteria already recognized as sources of foodborne illnesses have found new modes of transmission. While many illnesses from *E. coli* O157:H7 occur from eating insufficiently cooked hamburger, these bacteria have also been found more recently in other foods, such as salami, raw milk, apple cider, and lettuce.

Fifth, some pathogens are far more resistant than expected to longstanding food-processing and storage techniques previously believed to provide some protection against the growth of bacteria. For example, some bacterial pathogens (such as *Yersinia* and *Listeria*) can continue to grow in food under refrigeration.

Finally, according to CDC officials, virulent strains of well-known bacteria have continued to emerge. For example, one such pathogen, *E. coli* O104:H21, is another potentially deadly strain of *E. coli*. In 1994, CDC found this new strain in milk from a Montana dairy.

The costs of foodborne illnesses

While foodborne illnesses are often temporary, they can also result in more serious illnesses requiring hospitalization, long-term disability, and death. Although the overall cost of foodborne illnesses is not known, two

USDA estimates place some of the costs in the range of $5.6 billion to more than $22 billion per year. The first estimate, covering only the portion related to the medical costs and productivity losses of seven specific pathogens, places the costs in the range of $5.6 billion to $9.4 billion. The second, covering only the value of avoiding deaths from five specific pathogens, places the costs in the range of $6.6 billion to $22 billion.

Although often mild, foodborne illnesses can lead to more serious illnesses and death.

Although often mild, foodborne illnesses can lead to more serious illnesses and death. For example, in a small percentage of cases, foodborne infections can spread through the bloodstream to other organs, resulting in serious long-term disability or death. Serious complications can also result when diarrhetic infections resulting from foodborne pathogens act as a triggering mechanism in susceptible individuals, causing an illness such as reactive arthritis to flare up. In other cases, no immediate symptoms may appear, but serious consequences may eventually develop. The likelihood of serious complications is unknown, but some experts estimate that about 2 to 3 percent of all cases of foodborne illness lead to serious consequences. For example:

• *E. coli* O157:H7 can cause kidney failure in young children and infants and is most commonly transmitted to humans through the consumption of undercooked ground beef. The largest reported outbreak in North America occurred in 1993 and affected over 700 people, including many children who ate undercooked hamburgers at a fast food restaurant chain. Fifty-five patients, including four children who died, developed a severe disease, Hemolytic Uremic Syndrome, which is characterized by kidney failure.

• *Salmonella* can lead to reactive arthritis, serious infections, and deaths. In recent years, outbreaks have been caused by the consumption of many different foods of animal origin, including beef, poultry, eggs, milk and dairy products, and pork. The largest outbreak, occurring in the Chicago area in 1985, involved over 16,000 laboratory-confirmed cases and an estimated 200,000 total cases. Some of these cases resulted in reactive arthritis. For example, one institution that treated 565 patients from this outbreak confirmed that 13 patients had developed reactive arthritis after consuming contaminated milk. In addition, 14 deaths may have been associated with this outbreak.

• *Listeria* can cause meningitis and stillbirths and is fatal in 20 to 40 percent of cases. All foods may contain these bacteria, particularly poultry and dairy products. Illnesses from this pathogen occur mostly in single cases rather than in outbreaks. The largest outbreak in North America occurred in 1985 in Los Angeles, largely in pregnant women and their fetuses. More than 140 cases of illness were reported, including at least 13 cases of meningitis. At least 48 deaths, including 20 stillbirths or miscarriages, were attributed to the outbreak. Soft cheese produced in a contaminated factory was confirmed as the source.

• *Campylobacter* may be the most common precipitating factor for

Guillain-Barre syndrome, which is now one of the leading causes of paralysis from disease in the United States. *Campylobacter* infections occur in all age groups, with the greatest incidence in children under 1 year of age. The vast majority of cases occur individually, primarily from poultry, not during outbreaks. Researchers estimate that 4,250 cases of Guillain-Barre syndrome occur each year and that about 425 to 1,275 of these cases are preceded by *Campylobacter* infections.

While the overall annual cost of foodborne illnesses is unknown, the studies we reviewed estimate that it is in the billions of dollars. The range of estimates among the studies is wide, however, principally because of uncertainty about the number of cases of foodborne illness and related deaths. Other differences stem from the differences in the analytical approach used to prepare the estimate. Some economists attempt to estimate the costs related to medical treatment and lost wages (the cost-of-illness method); others attempt to estimate the value of reducing the incidence of illness or loss of life (the willingness-to-pay method). Two recent estimates demonstrate these differences in analytical approach.

In the first, USDA's Economic Research Service (ERS) used the cost-of-illness approach to estimate that the 1993 medical costs and losses in productivity resulting from seven major foodborne pathogens ranged between $5.6 billion and $9.4 billion. Of these costs, $2.3 billion to $4.3 billion were the estimated medical costs for the treatment of acute and chronic illnesses, and $3.3 billion to $5.1 billion were the productivity losses from the long-term effects of foodborne illnesses.

CDC, FDA, and ERS economists stated that these estimates may be low for several reasons. First, the cost-of-illness approach generates low values for reducing health risks to children and the elderly because these groups have low earnings and hence low productivity losses. Second, this approach does not recognize the value that individuals may place on (and pay for) feeling healthy, avoiding pain, or using their free time. In addition, not all of the 30 pathogens associated with foodborne illnesses were included.

In the second analysis, ERS used the willingness-to-pay method to estimate the value of preventing deaths for five of the seven major pathogens (included in the first analysis) at $6.6 billion to $22 billion in 1992. The estimate's range reflected the range in the estimated number of deaths, 1,646 to 3,144, and the range in the estimated value of preventing a death, $4 million to $7 million. Although these estimated values were higher than those resulting from the first approach, they may have also understated the economic cost of foodborne illnesses because they did not include an estimate of the value of preventing nonfatal illnesses and included only five of the seven major pathogens examined in the first analysis.

Responding to food safety threats

The federal food safety system has evolved over the years as changes were made to address specific health threats and respond to new technological developments. Often such changes occurred in reaction to a major outbreak of foodborne illness when consumers, industry, regulatory agencies, and the Congress agreed that actions needed to be taken. The system has been slow to respond to changing health risks, for a variety of reasons, including a lack of comprehensive data on the levels of risk and the sources of contamination.

While current data indicate that the risk of foodborne illnesses is significant, public health and food safety officials believe that these data do not identify the level of risk, the sources of contamination, and the populations most at risk in sufficient detail. According to these experts, the current voluntary reporting system does not provide sufficient data on the prevalence and sources of foodborne illnesses. There are no specific national requirements for reporting on foodborne pathogens. According to CDC, states do not (1) report on all pathogens of concern, (2) usually identify whether food was the source of the illness, or (3) identify many of the outbreaks or individual cases of foodborne illness that occur.

Consequently, according to CDC, FDA, and FSIS, public health officials cannot precisely determine the level of risk from known pathogens or be certain that they can detect the existence and spread of new pathogens in a timely manner. They also cannot identify all factors that put the public at risk or all types of food or situations in which microbial contamination is likely to occur. Finally, without better data, regulators cannot assess the effectiveness of their efforts to control the level of pathogens in food.

Structural problems . . . adversely affect the federal food safety system.

More uniform and comprehensive data on the number and causes of foodborne illnesses could form the basis of more effective control strategies. A better system for monitoring the extent of foodborne illnesses would actively seek out specific cases and would include outreach to physicians and clinical laboratories. CDC demonstrated the effectiveness of such an outreach effort when it conducted a long-term study, initiated in 1986, to determine the number of cases of illness caused by *Listeria*. This study showed that a lower rate of illness caused by *Listeria* occurred between 1989 and 1993 during the implementation of food safety programs designed to reduce the prevalence of *Listeria* in food.

In July 1995, CDC, FDA, and FSIS began a comprehensive effort to track the major bacterial pathogens that cause foodborne illnesses. These agencies are collaborating with the state health departments in five areas across the country to better determine the incidence of infection with *Salmonella, E. coli* O157:H7, and other foodborne bacteria and to identify the sources of diarrheal illness from *Salmonella* and *E. coli* O157:H7.[3] Initially, FDA provided $378,000 and FSIS provided $500,000 through CDC to the five locations for 6 months. For fiscal year 1996, FSIS provided $1 million and FDA provided $300,000. CDC provides overall management and coordination and facilitates the development of technical expertise at the sites through its established relationships with the state health departments.

CDC and the five sites will use the information to identify emerging foodborne pathogens and monitor the incidence of foodborne illness. FSIS will use the data to evaluate the effectiveness of new food safety programs and regulations to reduce foodborne pathogens in meat and poultry and assist in future program development. FDA will use the data to evaluate its efforts to reduce foodborne pathogens in seafood, dairy products, fruit, and vegetables.

The agencies believe that this effort should be a permanent part of a sound public health system. According to CDC, FDA, and FSIS officials, such projects must collect data over a number of years to identify national trends and evaluate the effectiveness of strategies to control pathogens in food. Funding was decreased (on an annualized basis) for this project in 1996, and these officials are concerned about the continuing availability of funding, in this era of budget constraints, to conduct this discretionary effort over the longer term.

Obstacles to improving food safety

While providing more comprehensive data would help federal food safety officials develop better control strategies, it would not address the structural problems that adversely affect the federal food safety system. As we previously testified to this Committee, the current system was not developed under any rational plan but evolved over many years to address specific health threats from particular food products and has not responded to changing health risks.[4] As a result, the food safety system is a patchwork of inconsistent approaches that weaken its effectiveness. For example, as we reported in June 1992, food products posing the same risk are subject to different rules, limited inspection resources are inefficiently used, and agencies must engage in extensive and often unsuccessful coordination activities in an attempt to address food safety issues.

While federal agencies have made progress in moving towards a scientific, risk-based inspection system, foods posing similar health risks, such as seafood, meat, and poultry, are still treated differently because of underlying differences in regulatory approach. For example, FDA's hazard analysis critical control point (HACCP) requirement for seafood processors differs from FSIS' proposed HACCP program for meat and poultry processors.[5] Under FSIS' proposal, meat and poultry plants would be required to conduct microbiological tests to verify the overall effectiveness of their critical controls and processing systems.[6] In comparison, FDA's HACCP program for seafood products has no testing requirement. Furthermore, because the frequency of inspection is based on the agencies' regulatory approach, some foods may be receiving too much attention, while other foods may not be receiving enough. FSIS will conduct oversight of industries that use HACCP programs on a daily basis and will continue to inspect every meat and poultry carcass. Conversely, FDA will inspect seafood plants about once every 2 years and will only inspect other food plants under its jurisdiction an average of about once every 8 years. As we stated in our June 1992 report, such widely differing inspection frequencies for products posing similar risk is an inefficient use of limited federal inspection resources.

Moreover, federal agencies are often slow to address emerging food safety concerns because of fragmented jurisdictions and responsibilities. For example, in April 1992, we reported that jurisdictional questions, disagreement about corrective actions, and poor coordination between FDA and USDA had hindered the federal government's efforts to control *Sal-*

monella in eggs for over 5 years.' At that time, we stated that the continuing nature of such problems indicated that the food safety structure—with federal agencies having split and concurrent jurisdictions—had a systemic problem. The system's fragmented structure limited the government's ability to deal effectively with a major outbreak of foodborne disease, especially when such an outbreak required joint agency action.

Today, federal agencies are concerned with the potential impact on public health posed by Bovine Spongiform Encephalopathy (the so-called mad cow disease), which was the subject of your May 10, 1996, hearing. Because there is still no single, uniform food safety system, jurisdiction remains split between agencies. Ironically, FSIS is responsible for the safety of meat products sold to the public, but is not responsible for preventing cattle from being given feeds that could endanger public health. FDA is responsible.

Notes

1. *Food Safety: Information on Foodborne Illnesses* (GAO/RCED-96-96, May 8, 1996).

2. *Food Safety and Quality: Uniform, Risk-Based Inspection System Needed to Ensure Safe Food Supply* (GAO/RCED-92-152, June 26, 1992).

3. The areas are (1) the greater metropolitan area of Atlanta, (2) an area that is comprised of two northern California counties, (3) an area that is comprised of two Connecticut counties, (4) the state of Minnesota, and (5) the state of Oregon.

4. *Food Safety: A Unified, Risk-Based Food Safety System Needed* (GAO/T-RCED-94-223, May 25, 1994).

5. *Food Safety: New Initiatives Would Fundamentally Alter the Existing System* (GAO/RCED-96-81, Mar. 27, 1996).

6. *Meat and Poultry Inspection: Impact of USDA's Food Safety Proposal on State Agencies and Small Plants* (GAO/RCED-95-228, June 30, 1995) and *Analysis of HACCP Costs and Benefits* (GAO/RCED-96-62R, Feb. 29, 1996).

7. *Food Safety and Quality: Salmonella Control Efforts Show Need for More Coordination* (GAO/RCED-92-69, Apr. 21, 1992).

3

Factory Farming Threatens Food Safety

Nicols Fox, interviewed by Jim Motavalli

Jim Motavalli is the editor of E: The Environmental Magazine. *Nicols Fox is a journalist and the author of* Spoiled: The Dangerous Truth About a Food Chain Gone Haywire.

Food-borne illnesses are often the result of factory farming, the mass production of animals for food. The unsafe techniques used at these farms can often lead to contaminated hamburger, vegetables, and eggs. Hamburger is ground from many different cows, so one contaminated cow can infect a significant amount of meat. Animal waste can contaminate meat and vegetables. Unclean commercial hen houses produce eggs that contain the salmonella bacteria. Consumers can reduce the threat of food-borne illnesses by purchasing organic products.

Like a lot of other Americans, journalist Nicols Fox, a former editor at the *Washington Journalism Review* and a correspondent for *The Economist*, first heard about the deadly E. coli O[sub157]:H[sub7] bacteria in 1993. That was the year it attacked a group of Northwestern children, all of whom had eaten hamburgers at area Jack in the Box restaurants. Four of them died.

Originally an art critic, Fox found herself increasingly drawn into the E. coli case. "At first I thought Jack in the Box was just an anomaly," she says, "but after checking with the Centers for Disease Control, I found that it wasn't just isolated on the west coast—it was happening all over. Here was a fascinating story, a new bacterium that had somehow gotten into the food supply. Finding out how that happened became my obsession."

With the writing of her 1997 book, *Spoiled: The Dangerous Truth About a Food Chain Gone Haywire* (Penguin), Fox answered her questions about E. coli, but she also looked at other frightening pathogens that have invaded our food supply. These include Salmonella and Campylobacter, both of which have become almost omnipresent in poultry; and "mad cow" disease, which has invaded British beef and killed a dozen people in England.

Reprinted from Jim Motavalli, "Nicols Fox: Interview," E: The Environmental Magazine, May/June 1998, with the permission of E/The Environmental Magazine; subscription department: P.O. Box 2047, Marion, OH 43306. Telephone: (815) 734-1242. Subscriptions are $20 per year.

Fox is convinced that we can get these dangerous contaminants out of our food supply, and that Sweden's model programs of scrupulous cleaning and disinfecting show how it can be done. "Over here we're trying to deal with the problem through meat irradiation and other solutions, instead of attacking it at its source," says Fox. "We know what factors in chicken rearing, for instance, are responsible for Salmonella outbreaks. Some reforms have been made but, unfortunately, the U.S. Department of Agriculture (USDA) doesn't have the authority to order sweeping changes."

Fox, who lives in rural Maine, is working on a new book, *It Was Probably Something You Ate: A Practical Guide to Avoiding and Surviving Food-Borne Disease.*

Consumers and food safety

E: Spoiled is a very scary book about the ways in which modern agricultural and factory farming methods have left us with a food system that is dangerously contaminated. Maybe you could start with an overview of what you found.

FOX: First of all, I found that it was really very complicated. Why are we having all of these cases of food-borne illness? The answer lies in modern processing and factory farming. They both contribute, but the consumer also has a hand in it as well. There are many factors. We have changed our entire relationship to food. We've changed how we produce it, how we process it, how we distribute it. We've also changed what we cook, how we cook it, and how we buy it.

For instance, consumers want fresh fruits and vegetables all year-round. That means the produce has to come from all over the world, and it does. If you go to your local supermarket, the fruits and vegetables may come from 26 different countries. Every time we consume that produce, we are actually consuming the environment in which those foods were produced. We are consuming the quality of the water and the soil, and the sanitary conditions of the people who pick and pack them.

One of the things that scared me most was what you wrote about meat. You describe an incredible amount of contamination in, for instance, poultry. You say that 99 percent of chickens were found by the USDA in a sample to be contaminated with generic E. coli bacteria, indicating fecal contamination. And one E. coli O[sub157]:H[sub7]-infected cow can contaminate 16 tons of hamburger. Also, 72 percent of chickens in one study were found to be contaminated with Salmonella. If 99 percent of chickens are contaminated with generic E. coli, and 72 percent infected with Salmonella, how dangerous is that to people, assuming they buy chicken at the supermarket and they cook it properly? It puts an incredible onus on the cooking process.

It certainly does. Cooking can kill these microbes and render the food safe for you to eat, but there's also a danger that you will cross-contaminate other things in the kitchen. Take chicken, for instance. Virtually all of the chickens we buy are contaminated with something called Campylobacter, which you may have never heard of. Yet it is the most frequent cause of diarrheal disease in most parts of this country. If we are cooking our chicken thoroughly, why are so many people getting sick? Some studies have shown that the person most likely to become sick is the person preparing the chicken, because it's on their hands—it may also get on the counters, on the cutting boards, et cetera. You have to be very careful not to transfer the bacteria that are on these products into things that you are going to eat without cooking, like salad ingredients.

You note that when cooking hamburgers on the grill, you have to be careful not to put the cooked hamburgers on the platter that also held the uncooked hamburgers. You can re-contaminate the meat that way.

That's exactly right. Anything that you have touched with that uncooked meat product should be washed before it touches a cooked meat product, and that would be something like a spatula. People don't even think of that. There are actually cases where people have become seriously ill because of the spatula that was used to transfer an uncooked, then a cooked burger. To me it is really asking the consumer to operate a kind of biohazard lab, and that's too complicated for me. I just stopped bringing meat into the kitchen.

Further food risks

You're what you call a "reluctant" vegetarian.

I'm sad to say that, really, I've always enjoyed meat in my diet. The first thing I gave up was hamburger. I think I wouldn't have been so concerned about it if it were something I'd ground myself. But hamburger now is mass produced in places like Iowa or Nebraska from all the scraps left over from cutting meat. As you've already pointed out, one contaminated cow can contaminate a significant amount of meat, because hamburger may contain a hundred different animals from four different countries. Some of these animals may be dairy cattle carrying infections.

You're essentially saying what Oprah Winfrey said. Would you go so far as to recommend that people not eat hamburger?

I think everyone has to make their own decision. If you really are a hamburger fanatic and are so unwise as to want to eat it rare, then you probably ought to go to the grocery store, buy a chuck steak and bring it home. Grind it up yourself in your own clean grinder, which you make sure to wash thoroughly afterwards. I know that's a lot of trouble, but when I say that, I'm surprised at the number of people who say, 'My grandmother used to do that.' I think that we've become very complacent about our food. We don't want to give it any time or attention, and we put it so low on our scale of values. It's really become no more than a refueling process.

One of the implications of what you're saying is that you are not necessarily safe if you're a vegetarian. Vegetables and fruits are easily contaminated. If you buy, say, a commercial supermarket salad packaged in a bag, I imagine it is very easy for that salad to become contaminated.

Well, yes. We have to ask, what was this lettuce washed in? Who cut it up for us? I think it's ironic that we turned a lot of food safety activity over to the lowest-paid workers in our entire economy. Some of those salad bags come labeled "triple-washed" and the implication is clearly that these foods are ready for the salad bowl. And yet, I took a bag of that "triple-washed" lettuce, washed it and found about a tablespoon of dirt in the bottom of the pan. Not enough consumers are aware that just about everything you eat needs to be washed, and even that's not a guarantee. But I have to go back and say that you are more likely to confront these disease-causing microorganisms on animal products, which are contaminated by animal waste. Fecal matter gets onto the meat during slaughter, and there are various things that occur in processing that can exacerbate it. Vegetables are less likely to be contaminated with animal waste, but it can happen.

Egg safety

Let's talk about Salmonella and eggs a little bit. You wrote that cooking eggs the ways millions of Americans like them, sunny side up, for instance, doesn't necessarily kill Salmonella.

That's right. These were tests carried out in England. What has happened to the egg is nothing less than a tragedy, because the egg is such a versatile food. I was looking in my master French cook book and found 123 main course dishes that contained egg. If you cooked them the way we are now directed to cook them, there would only be 23 of those dishes left, an 83 percent decline. In these English tests, they inoculated eggs with Salmonella and then checked to see how hard they had to be before the Salmonella died. And they found that only scrambling them quickly at a very high heat, boiling them for nine minutes or longer, or frying them until the yolk solidified was enough. When the Minnesota Public Health Department did a survey of people who had Salmonella infections, the great majority of them had eaten undercooked eggs, just in the ordinary way many of us had: Sunny side up, poached or something like that.

Why are we having all of these cases of food-borne illness? The answer lies in modern processing and factory farming.

How could we effectively rid ourselves of Salmonella contamination?

I eat organic eggs from a small producer in Massachusetts. They are fed grain, not the kind of chicken feed that may contain ground-up chickens and animal protein which may contain bacteria. The chickens go outside. And they don't get antibiotics, which is another factor in stressing these birds. Most importantly, though, these birds are tested three times in their life for Salmonella and the tests have come up negative.

Most eggs in the United States are raised in factory operations where you have something like 70,000 birds in a huge hen house. How do we mainstream the kind of conditions you're talking about?

We'd have to change the way we're producing eggs, because all of the factors in intensive production have contributed in one way or another. For instance, we breed chickens for producing eggs on a very regular basis—we select for the best producers. So if you go into a commercial hen house, all the chickens are actually like clones, as close as you can get without actually cloning them. This means that they're all identically susceptible to disease. The feed that they get may well be contaminated; it often is. They are fed antibiotics, which not only selects for certain bacterial strains, it seems to lead to antibiotic resistance in these strains. Rats and mice may get in the house and run on the conveyer belts that feed these birds and then take away their eggs. They may run from house to house so that disease may spread between the houses. The water may be dirty. All of these factors are going to contribute to the birds being susceptible to certain diseases, and in one way or another, they can pass them on to us.

Reconsidering food policies

Unfortunately, what I see facing the world is an imperative to produce food intensively because of population increases. The U.S. is likely to double its population by 2100. Many countries have doubled or tripled their populations very recently. Just to keep up with feeding people, some observers say we more or less have to go with intensive crop management, using a lot of pesticides and intensive animal agriculture.

That's operating on the assumption that the only way we can produce this amount of food is through intensive farming, and I don't believe that is necessarily true. Organic farmers are finding that it is not as difficult as it originally was thought to produce high-quality, high-yield food in a competitive situation.

I think we also need to look closely at the things that are making disease worse. For instance, we might have more of a variety in chickens in these houses. We might have smaller houses, and more of them. We might not have them connected with conveyer belts, which can spread disease. The houses should certainly be kept clean, and the animals need clean food and water—that's only common sense.

We in the United States have the cheapest food in the world, and that's been a matter of USDA policy. We need to look again at that policy and see whether it is truly helpful to us as a nation. It may be resulting in more food-borne disease, which just shifts the true cost elsewhere. That's not to say that more expensive food is always safer, because it certainly isn't. Look at the people who got sick from expensive imported raspberries. There are many factors creating this increase in food-borne disease. We just need to take a saner approach.

4

Organic Farming Is a Source of Unsafe Food

Dennis T. Avery

Dennis T. Avery is a senior fellow of the Hudson Institute, a not-for-profit organization that advocates practical approaches to public policy research. He is also the director of Hudson's Center for Global Food Issues and the author of Saving the Planet With Pesticides and Plastic: The Environmental Triumph of High-Yield Farming.

Despite the claims of organic farmers and their supporters, organic food is more dangerous than produce grown by conventional farming methods. Organic produce is unsafe because its farmers use bacteria-laden animal manure for fertilizer, they do not apply preservatives or chemicals that will remove dangerous bacteria, and they often do not utilize safe composting methods. These dangers are not widely reported, however, because the organic food lobby is politically powerful.

According to data compiled by the U.S. Centers for Disease Control (CDC), people who eat organic and "natural" foods are eight times as likely as the rest of the population to be attacked by a deadly new strain of E. coli bacteria (0157: H7). This new E. coli is attacking tens of thousands of people per year, all over the world. It is causing permanent liver and kidney damage in many of its victims. The CDC recorded 2,471 confirmed cases of E. coli 0157: H7 in 1996 and estimated that it is causing at least 250 deaths per year in the United States alone.

The increasing threat of contamination

Consumers of organic food are also more likely to be attacked by a relatively new, more virulent strain of the infamous salmonella bacteria. Salmonella was America's biggest food-borne death risk until the new E. coli 0157 came along.

Organic food is more dangerous than conventionally grown produce because organic farmers use animal manure as the major source of fertil-

Reprinted from Dennis T. Avery, "The Hidden Dangers in Organic Food," *American Outlook*, Fall 1998, by permission of the Hudson Institute.

31

izer for their food crops. Animal manure is the biggest reservoir of these nasty bacteria that are afflicting and killing so many people.

Organic farmers compound the contamination problem through their reluctance to use antimicrobial preservatives, chemical washes, pasteurization, or even chlorinated water to rid their products of dangerous bacteria. One organic grower summed up the community's attitude as follows: "Pasteurization has only been around a hundred years or so; what do they think people did before that?"

The answer is simple. They died young.

In truth, until the last few years the threat of food-borne bacteria was relatively mild in the U.S. It was prudent to refrigerate one's food and wash one's hands before preparing food or eating, and those simple procedures kept food-borne illnesses to a minimum. On occasion, neglect of these rules would cause a family to suffer severe stomach aches. And every year a few weak individuals—the very young, the very old, or those who were already quite ill—would die from exposure to food-borne bacteria.

But the new E. coli attacks even the strong. It inflicts permanent damage on internal organs. It even kills healthy adults. The new salmonella is nearly as dangerous.

The dangers of organic foods

As these lethal new bacteria spread, organic foods have clearly become the deadliest food choice. Put simply, animal manure is too dangerous to use on food crops if there is any alternative whatever. To eat produce grown with animal fertilizer is like playing Russian roulette with your family's dinner table. It only takes one contaminated food product to bring on a tragedy.

"I was really horrified that something I felt was so wholesome and so healthy and so safe for my children could really almost kill them," said Rita Bernstein, a Connecticut housewife. In 1996, two of Bernstein's three daughters suffered E. coli 0157 attacks that were traced to organic lettuce. Halee, the younger daughter, is still suffering from reduced kidney function and vision problems. Bernstein is grateful that her daughters are still alive. "There are a lot of families out there that don't have their Halees," she says.

The new reality is quite sobering. Organic and "natural" food producers supply only about 1 percent of the nation's food, but the Centers for Disease Control have traced approximately 8 percent of the confirmed E. coli 0157 cases to such foods. *Consumer Reports* found much higher levels of salmonella on free-range chickens than on conventionally raised ones. Many other organic foods also pose higher salmonella risks than "supermarket" foods. To be sure, most strains of salmonella are mild and are easily killed by cooking one's food adequately. But the new salmonella, S. typhimurium, is far stronger than other varieties. Infection often proves fatal. The CDC estimates that there are up to four million cases of salmonella poisoning per year in the U.S., and it has identified one-fourth of the culture-confirmed cases as the more virulent S. typhimurium.

As if that were not frightening enough, organic and "natural" food consumers also face increased risk of illness from toxins produced by fungi—and some of these toxins are carcinogenic. Refusing to use artificial pesticides, organic farmers allow their crop fields to suffer more damage from insects and rodents, which creates openings through which fungi can enter the fruits and seeds. The U.S. Food and Drug Administration (FDA) regularly tests samples of various foods for such dangers, and it routinely finds high levels of these natural toxins in organically grown produce. It found, for instance, that organic crops have higher rates of infestation by aflatoxin, one of the most virulent carcinogens known to man. Unfortunately, the FDA has issued no public warnings about these risks so far.

The organic-food sector stresses the "natural" production of foods and beverages—even to the point of refusing to pasteurize milk and fruit juices. As a result, many people become seriously ill after consuming products they mistakenly believe are purer than other foods. For instance, in 1996 E. coli 0157 sickened more than seventy people who contracted it from unpasteurized apple juice produced by the Odwalla Juice Company. One young girl in Colorado died because of this. Odwalla was fined more than $1 million in the case and now pasteurizes its juice. But more than 1,500 other companies still cater to the "natural means raw" idea by selling unpasteurized beverages that can prove deadly.

Even without pesticides and pasteurization, producers could render their organic and natural foods safe through a well-known process called irradiation. Irradiation uses low levels of gamma radiation to kill bacteria, and the process also preserves the freshness of foods such as strawberries and chicken. But when the U.S. Department of Agriculture (USDA) proposed an organic-food standard that would have allowed irradiation, the plan drew more than 200,000 angry protests from organic farmers and caterers. In response, the USDA will reportedly eliminate irradiation from the final organic food standard. [Irradiation was removed in early 1999.]

Poor farming techniques

To be sure, it is an overstatement to say, as one physician recently did, that organic food is "grown in animal manure." Few organic farmers actually put fresh manure on their crops. Most of them compost the manure for several weeks before using it on their crops. But the composting guidelines have been fuzzy and are probably inadequate. A common rule of thumb is to compost for two months at 130 degrees F. or better. The bad news is that a study by Dr. Dean Cliver of the University of California at Davis found that the deadly new E. coli 0157 bacteria can live at least seventy days in a compost pile—and it probably takes an extended period at 160-degree heat to kill it.

Few organic farmers use thermometers to check the safety of their compost piles, or even keep accurate records on how long a given mass of compost has been sitting. For most organic farmers, management of their natural fertilizer is a casual matter of shifting compost piles around with a tractor-mounted front-end loader.

The real surprise is that nobody is telling the public about the new dangers from organic food, or trying to persuade organic farmers to reduce these risks. Activist groups, government, and the press—all of which have shown no reluctance to organize crusades about matters such as global warming, tobacco addiction, and the use of pesticides—are allow-

`

ing organic farmers to endanger their customers without any publicity whatever. A press corps eager to find headline-worthy dangers would long ago have exposed any other farmers guilty of so blatantly and unnecessarily endangering the public. And other farmers would certainly have been condemned, or even closed down, by government regulators.

Organic foods, however, are politically favored. The Green lobby self-righteously protects them because it urgently wants the public to perceive organic farming as an environmentally benign alternative to the use of pesticides and chemical fertilizers. I criticized organic farming on a Canadian Broadcasting Corporation program, and the network was peppered with protest calls before the program even went on the air!

Organic food is more dangerous than conventionally grown produce.

Even newspaper food editors still tell their readers that organic food is chic, healthy, and "earth-friendly." In general, the U.S. press has been blithely abetting the scare tactics of the environmental movement for decades, and the food writers pride themselves on being at least as "green" as their colleagues on the news pages.

With truly mind-numbing aggressiveness, the organic farming advocates have even gone so far as to claim that "industrial farming" created E. coli 0157. They argue that consumers should protect themselves by buying organic products from local farmers, a "recommendation" that blatantly serves their own self-interest. The truth is, no one knows where the new E. coli strain came from, but we do know that bacteria are constantly mutating as a natural consequence of their rapid reproduction. Allowing bacteria to proliferate, as organic farmers do, is not the way to minimize mutations.

Ineffective government responses

Federal regulators have largely been cowed into silence. The intensity with which organic-farming believers and eco-activists defend their old-fashioned type of agriculture rivals the intensity of the religious fanatic. For instance, one consumer said, "I think trying to eliminate the poisons and pesticides from our food is a great way to eliminate the chemical industry's destruction of the earth." As a consequence of such attitudes, the CDC has neglected its responsibility to warn the public about the newly increased dangers of organic foods. One CDC doctor—Dr. Robert Tauxe, Chief of the CDC's Food-Borne Diseases Branch—wrote an article in the *Journal of the American Medical Association* (May 8, 1997) highlighting the dangers of "organically grown, unprocessed foods produced without pesticides or preservatives." The CDC was promptly flooded with angry phone calls from passionate believers in organic farming. The doctor now says that he "doesn't know" whether organic food is more dangerous than conventionally produced food. The CDC has refused to grant interviews on the subject.

With similar obtuseness, the U.S. Environmental Protection Agency

(EPA) has issued a draft of a new consumer brochure highlighting the unproven "dangers" from pesticide residues—and recommending organic foods. But after forty years and billions of dollars in research, scientists are still looking for the first victim of pesticide residues, whereas the new E. coli strain attacked thousands of Americans last year. Many of these victims suffered permanent internal organ damage, and hundreds of them died. The EPA's draft brochure on pesticide residues simply appears to reflect the antipesticide biases of the agency's administrator, Carol Browner, and her political patron, Vice President Al Gore.

Other federal agencies have displayed the same bias. The Food and Drug Administration, for instance, has failed to issue any warnings to consumers about the higher levels of natural toxins their researchers regularly find in organic foods. And the Department of Agriculture, which employs some of the world's best food scientists, goes out of its way to court the organic-farming supporters and allied eco-activists, and makes a strenuous effort to find good things to say about "alternative agriculture."

"Natural food" proponents claim that organic farming is "earth-friendly," but it's not. The ugly secret of organic farming is that its yields are only about half as high as those of mainstream farmers. Approximately one-third of the average organic farm is not planted to marketable crops at all; it is planted to green manure crops (such as clover) to build up the nitrogen fertility of the soil. If the organic farmers gave up animal manure as a nitrogen source, the percentage of land they keep in green manure crops would have to become even higher. Mainstream farmers take their nitrogen from the air, through an industrial process that requires no land to be taken from nature.

Also, the organic farmers suffer higher losses from destruction by pests. They expect it. Books on organic farming tell their readers to live with it. "I'm lucky to get half as much yield from my organic acres as from my regular fields," said the manager of a 50,000-acre cooperative farm in England. His experience is confirmed by numerous studies from a dozen different countries.

Organic farming is not the answer

For all these reasons, widespread organic farming is simply not a viable option at this time. The first consequence of a global shift to organic farming would be the plowdown of at least six-million square miles of wildlife habitat to make up for the lower yields of organic production. That is more than the total land area of the United States.

Agriculture already takes up 36 percent of the world's land surface. (All the world's cities cover only 1.5 percent.) A world with a peak population of 8.5 billion affluent people in 2050 will need at least 2.5 times as much farm output as we have today.

Absent a worldwide catastrophe involving billions of human deaths, this demand is inevitable. We will not be able to count on people to change their diets and accept less protein. There is no global trend toward vegetarianism today, nor any sign of one. In America, for example, less than 4 percent of the population is vegetarian, and 95 percent of U.S. vegetarians consume milk, cheese, eggs, and other expensive calories. Less than 0.05 percent of the affluent people in the world give up livestock products completely.

In fact, the worldwide trend is in the opposite direction. Countries such as China, India, and South Korea are leading the biggest surge in demand for meat and milk the world has ever seen. It is now probably too late to save wildlands by preventing people from acquiring a taste for meat and milk, and there is certainly no sign of mass conversions to vegetarianism around the globe.

If the world does not triple the yields on the high-quality land currently in farming, we will pay the price not in human famine but in forests and wild meadows cleared to produce more meat, milk, and produce.

Widespread organic farming is simply not a viable option at this time.

Modern farm chemicals are not entirely without risk, but the hazards they pose to people and wildlife are near zero and declining. For instance, Captan, one of the pesticides on the Greenpeace hit list, is *one ten-millionth* as carcinogenic as ordinary drinking water. EPA Administrator Browner is trying to decertify an herbicide called atrazine because a few parts per billion turn up in some of our drinking water. But Browner's own staff concedes that to get above the "no-effect" level in the rat tests that ascertain cancer risk, you would have to drink 150,000 gallons of water per day for seventy years. And for nine months of the year you would have to add your own atrazine! The health risks of modern pesticides are minimal.

Nonetheless, advocates of organic farming like to ask, "What's more dangerous, pesticides or horse manure?" The answer may surprise them. Researchers are still looking for the first human death from pesticide residues, fifty years after DDT was introduced and thirty years after its use was banned in the United States, but manure is apparently claiming lives almost daily through bacterial contamination of organic food.

Nor do modern pesticides pose a significant risk to wildlife. They are more narrowly targeted, degrade more rapidly, and are better designed to avoid wildlife impact than the early, more persistent pesticides. Also, they are often used in integrated pest management systems to minimize the amount and frequency of treatments, and are applied with computer-calculated precision. The new glyphosate and sulfanylurea weed killers are no more toxic to birds and fish than table salt, and one tiny tablet treats an entire acre. Quite simply, when used properly these substances are not dangerous to anything but the pests they are designed to regulate.

Giving up pesticides would mean the certain destruction of millions of square miles of wildlands, much of it in the species-rich tropics. Because much of the world's biodiversity is in those lands, a move toward widespread organic farming would cost nature far more than the careful use of today's safe, narrowly targeted pesticides, high-powered seeds, and factory-produced fertilizers.

Organic food buyers are, unfortunately, twice losers: They and their families accept deadly risks from truly dangerous new food-borne microorganisms, and, at the same time, their choices increase the likelihood that the people of the next century will plow down massive tracts of wildlife habitat to make way for low-yield crops.

Unless the press and government agencies fulfill their obligation to warn people of the dangers of these foods, the number of such incidents will continue to rise. These risks are easy to overcome, but farmers and consumers must know the dangers and act accordingly.

5

Pesticides Are Safe

Alex Avery

Alex Avery is the director of research and education at the Center for Global Food Issues at the Hudson Institute, a public policy research organization.

Pesticides reduce contamination of the food supply, increase the availability of fresh produce, and do not pose health or environmental risks. Therefore, they are essential to farmers and society. The Environmental Protection Agency (EPA) should consider the benefits of pesticides and end its excessive regulation of these chemicals.

Why is the Environmental Protection Agency regulating pesticides as if it were a pole vaulting competition instead of requiring pesticides to simply be safe? The agency keeps raising the safety bar and crowing about how much it is improving public health. Yet the bar has now reached a ridiculous height. Increasing pesticide safety standards from one theoretical cancer case in a million to one in a billion provides no health benefit—especially since the EPA's means for calculating health risks vastly overestimates exposure and toxicity. And further increases in pesticide safety requirements are hurting public health.

It is no secret that the EPA is out to eliminate as many pesticides as it can. That has been a core goal of the agency ever since it was created by the Nixon administration in the midst of the uproar over dichlorodiphenyltrichloroethane (DDT). In 1993, the EPA's Administrator, Carol Browner, stated that "the most important thing is to reduce the overall use of pesticides. By doing that, we will automatically reduce risks and we won't have to spend all this time worrying about lots of complicated things."

Driving a pesticide off the market is an easy way for the EPA to win points with environmental activists and give a misinformed public the impression that it is working to improve public health. Naturally, the EPA chooses to ignore the decades of benefits from the use of pesticides and the adverse consequences from their cancellation.

Reprinted from Alex Avery, "Pesticide Pole Vaulting," *Regulation*, Spring 1998, with permission from the Cato Institute.

The benefits of pesticides

As the world struggles with the need to produce even more food from a finite amount of farmland, effective pesticides will become even more important. The EPA ignores the problems that banning pesticides will create.

First, pesticides reduce crop losses from pests. Having a wide array of pesticides available reduces production costs and increases the availability of fruits and vegetables. Increased consumption of fruits and vegetables radically cuts cancer risks and has been strongly recommended by numerous health organizations. Currently, less than 10 percent of Americans meet the recommended level of fruit and vegetable consumption. By narrowing the range of available pesticides, the EPA inadvertently discourages fruit and vegetable consumption.

Second, pesticides reduce contamination of the food supply with dangerous microorganisms and the toxins that they produce. Canceling pesticides and leaving crops without adequate protection could seriously increase the danger from those natural hazards. Even if there are alternative pesticides available to replace older ones that are cancelled, when the EPA reduces the number of safe pesticides it creates another danger. When farmers have only one or two pesticides available, the opportunity for pests to develop resistance to a pesticide increases dramatically. In those situations, farmers must use the same pesticide over and over and cannot effectively rotate chemicals with different modes of action. When combating the development of pest resistance, the wider the spectrum of available pesticides the better.

The health risks from pesticide residues have clearly demonstrated to be immeasurably small or nonexistent.

The EPA touts the added safety of newer pesticides, which are often more narrowly targeted against specific pests. While such pesticides reduce potential effects on nontarget species, the higher specificity also increases the risk of pest resistance. Those pesticides usually work by disrupting unique biochemical processes in the target pests. However, those processes are often easily adaptable, so pests may develop resistance to the pesticides quickly.

The older, broader-spectrum pesticides work by disrupting more central biological functions in pests, which is why they affect a wider range of organisms. And it is more difficult for organisms to develop resistance to such pesticides.

The EPA claims to favor integrated pest management strategies, but it resists the logic that a wide array of pest-killing chemicals is essential to achieve that end.

The EPA regulates on the unwritten assumption that no pesticide will ever prove itself safe enough. Thus it forces pesticide producers to comply with near-constant requests for additional and expensive safety testing of already-registered pesticides. The agency's insatiable appetite for such data is slowly driving pesticides with time-tested human health and environmental safety records off the market. Because they have proven difficult for pests to develop resistance against, even after long periods of use, the impact on agriculture of the loss of those particular pesticides will be especially great. Thus American farmers will have access to a dwindling number of relatively high-priced pesticides.

The costs of regulation

A laundry list of pesticides have been "voluntarily" pulled off the market in light of the growing regulatory burden. Among them is Dyfonate, a fungicide used by mint and potato growers, and Phosalone, an insecticide used by pecan growers. The loss of Captafol, a fungicide used by cherry and cranberry growers is responsible for the reduction in fresh market cranberries. Chloramben, an herbicide used on lettuce in Florida, was dropped from the market in the mid 1980s. Growers in that state spent nearly $2 million per year for the next decade to weed lettuce fields by hand before finally getting a new herbicide registration.

As an example of just how high continual registration costs can be, over $50 million has been spent during the last decade to maintain the registration of just one pesticide: atrazine. Widely used as a corn herbicide, atrazine was first registered for use almost forty years ago. It plays a vital role in the no-till and conservation tillage systems that have drastically reduced soil erosion and chemical and fertilizer runoff on millions of acres of American cropland. After some four decades of use, no health risk has been attributed to atrazine exposure. In fact, according to an internal review of its own data, the EPA concluded that atrazine is actually significantly safer than previously believed. Yet the testing demands on that product continue.

Ironically, many cancelled pesticides could pass the new safety tests. But the market for many of those pesticides is too small to support the high costs of additional safety testing, so manufacturers just throw in the towel. Pesticides like atrazine, that are used on the biggest selling crops, can, to some extent, absorb such costs because of the huge size of the pesticide market in those crops. But pesticides used on fruits and vegetables that are grown on a relatively small number of acres are vulnerable.

Higher standards are a misguided approach

Higher pesticide safety standards might be understandable if they lead to significant improvements in human health or environmental protection. But they do not.

The health risks from pesticide residues have clearly demonstrated to be immeasurably small or nonexistent. No medical or scientific organization has ever questioned the fact that the health benefits from consuming fruits and vegetables vastly outweigh any theoretical health risk from pesticide residues. (Those issues must be discussed in terms of theoretical risk because no one has ever demonstrated any actual risks.)

Further, the adverse effects of pesticides on the environment are virtually nonexistent. When real problems do exist, they are usually limited and correctable. For example, Furadan 15G, a granular soil insecticide, was found to be killing birds, including secondary poisonings of endangered bald eagles in many states. In response, the pesticide producers voluntarily pulled the product from the market in states with sensitive bird populations. Most environmental damage from pesticides is confined to accidental spills of concentrated chemicals and contamination of industrial sites, not to their regular use on crops.

The EPA is now implementing the Food Quality Protection Act of 1996. The new law incorporates several provisions that will accelerate the cancellation of safe and effective pesticides.

Pesticides will now be grouped by their "mode of action." For example, if pesticide A and pesticide B both suppress the same enzyme system, risk-wise they will be treated as if they were one pesticide. Thus, residues of pesticides A and B will essentially be treated as residues of each other. However, because the allowable risk thresholds for each pesticide will not be combined and will remain the same, pesticides A and B will essentially share the risk threshold for only one pesticide.

Obviously that means that many pesticides will exceed their current theoretical risk allotment and will have to be cancelled. With more realistic exposure data, instead of the worst-case exposure assumptions the EPA has often used by default in the past, some pesticides may remain on the market. But the additional testing will certainly reveal crop uses with higher theoretical risk exposures, and those uses will likely disappear. Fruits and vegetables will be hardest hit. Products used not just by commercial farmers but also by private consumers are likely to be affected. Carbaryl for example, the active ingredient in the widely used garden insecticide Sevin and diazinon, a common lawn insecticide, might be pulled from the market.

Additionally, the EPA now has the discretion to increase the safety factors it adds to allowable pesticide exposures to "protect infants and children." Environmental and public health groups are already pushing for an across the board application of those additional safety factors. If additional safety factors are widely imposed, even more pesticides and specific crop uses will be squeezed off the market.

All in all, the end result of the EPA's policies will leave farmers and society with drastically fewer pesticides. And that will be bad for our health and the environment.

6

Pesticides Cause Significant Health Problems

Martin Bourque and Ingrid Bekkers

Martin Bourque is the Sustainable Agriculture Program Director at Food First, also known as the Institute for Food and Development Policy. Ingrid Bekkers is a former research intern at Food First. Food First is a think tank that works to find the causes and solutions to hunger and poverty.

The use of pesticides in farming creates serious health risks. These ill effects include cancer, liver dysfunction, and abnormalities in the reproductive system. Pesticides cause these problems by disrupting the human body's endocrine and hormone system. The U.S. government ignored these dangers when it passed the Food Quality Protection Act in 1996, which weakens pesticide regulation.

Q: What do androgynous alligators, and dolphin distemper have to do with human breast and prostate cancer?
   A: They're all involved in new studies focused on the unseen and previously unstudied impacts of pesticides.
   We've known since *Silent Spring*[1], that pesticides accumulate in the food chain and cause cancer, and that we need to keep residue levels in our food low. But the new findings brought to public attention in *Our Stolen Future*,[2] suggest that pesticides have much more dramatic effects at much lower doses than previously suspected. In fact, these findings may be so grave as to question the entire notion of using pesticides to produce food.

Pesticide research

As it becomes clear that many developmental and reproductive disorders are caused by the complex interactions of multiple pesticides and our hormone systems, a whole new area of pesticide research and policy discussion is emerging.[3] New studies are showing that pesticides have many more dangerous health impacts than just causing cancer. More alarming are the potential synergistic effects when several pesticides interact.
   Rachel Carson's *Silent Spring* forewarned us of health and environ-

Reprinted from Martin Bourque and Ingrid Bekkers, "Pesticides: New Discoveries Reveal Greater Threat to Human Health," *Food First Backgrounder*, Summer 1997, with permission from Food First.

mental impacts, and brought pesticide use under public scrutiny for the first time in the early 1960s.[4] Since then most of the research on the health consequences of pesticides has focused on cancer, trying to estimate the risk of individual pesticides on specific cancers as the basis for setting tolerance levels which government agencies feel are safe for human consumption.[5]

This research focus on cancer silenced the voices of scientists who were quietly studying the other pervasive and detrimental effects of pesticides on humans, animals, and the environment.[6] These scientists are now amassing new evidence revealing how complex the interactions between our body chemistry and pesticides really are,[7] and how multiple pesticides may magnify each other's effects.[8]

Unfortunately, U.S. pesticide policy is still focused on "risk management"—establishing tolerance levels for single pesticides, and does not yet include combinations of pesticides, or the cumulative impact of pesticides that function in the same ways. In this process, the Environmental Protection Agency (USEPA) sets a limit for how much of each pesticide is okay to have in your air, water, and food. Considering that over 700 pesticides are licensed for use in California alone,[9] we are all continually exposed to a mixture of hazardous chemical pesticides.

Concerns about pesticides

Concerns raised for the last 35 years have been of acute toxicity and chronic health problems. For years we have known that pesticides kill and permanently harm people who work directly with them. The acute effects of many pesticides are well documented; impacting the liver, kidneys, lungs, skin, eyes, and brain.[10] Long-term chronic effects on humans include a whole series of cancers, liver and kidney failure, sterility, neurological disorders and birth defects.[11]

Since *Silent Spring* we have known that pesticides which take a long time to break down in the environment accumulate in organisms as they move up the food chain. For example, the concentration of persistent organochlorine chemicals in lake water may be extremely low and well below the standards established by the U.S. EPA. But in algae in that same lake the concentration is increased up to 250 times. As the filter-feeding zooplankton eat the algae this concentration doubles; tiny shrimp eat so much zooplankton that the concentration jumps as high as 45,000 times that of the surrounding water. Fish eat the shrimp, and birds and other top predators eat the fish. These top predators have concentrations 25 million times[12] that found in the surrounding water. Humans are top predators and thus can accumulate relatively high concentrations of pesticides through the food supply.[13]

New evidence indicates that the proper functioning of the human body's most important regulatory system, the endocrine or hormone system, can be severely altered due to low level cumulative pesticide exposure. This system is directly linked to our neurological and immunological systems, further increasing the risks and potential impacts of pesticide exposure.[14] This evidence indicates that while low level exposure may not cause acute toxicity in adults, it can cause chronic reproductive immunological, and neurological disorders.[15] More alarming, low level exposure to unborn children can affect a wide range of developmental processes from reproductive system formation to brain function.[16]

Pesticides and the endocrine system

The endocrine system is the central, internal regulator of body chemistry, coordinating the 50 trillion cells in our body into a controlled and integrated organism. Without it our body cannot function. This system functions by releasing specific hormones, each from one of over a dozen glands, into the bloodstream. Key glands include the pituitary, thyroid, pancreas, adrenal, and testis in men, and ovaries in women. Hormones produced in these glands are released into the blood stream where many of them bind with specific proteins which help them arrive at their final destination. Once they reach specific receptor cells of their target organs they cause very specific reactions. In turn, these reactions either increase or decrease the amount of hormone released creating a self-regulating feedback loop. In this manner, the endocrine system controls an incredible number of biochemical functions ranging from the re-absorption of water in the kidneys to the regulation of blood sugar levels, from heart rate to responses of the immune system, and the timing of the menstrual cycle. Additionally, many important developmental processes are controlled by hormones making this system extremely important for unborn babies and developing children.

It is now clear that a wide variety of pesticides can distort the effects of hormones, sending the wrong messages to organs and disrupting the delicate balance of our internal biochemistry.[17] There are many stages in this process which are vulnerable to this disruption, and different periods in our life when we are more vulnerable to specific types of disruption. Additionally, each stage of the process may be disrupted by different mechanisms.

The most commonly discussed type of hormone disruption is called hormone mimicking. A synthetic chemical binds to a receptor cite and produces the normal response to a specific, but absent, hormone. This can create unsolicited responses from receptor cells and may accelerate or prolong responses that were begun by hormonal glands. Another mechanism is hormone blocking. Here a synthetic compound binds to the receptor cite and does not produce the effect of the hormone, but occupies the receptor cite making active hormones ineffective. Other mechanisms include disturbing the production process of the hormones, interfering with the helper or transport proteins, suppressing hormones and altering the breakdown of hormones once they have served their function.

Pesticides and reproduction

In the last fifty years, human sperm count may have decreased nearly 50%,[18] prostate cancer has skyrocketed 154%,[19] testicular cancer has nearly doubled,[20] and the incidence of breast cancer has increased by one percent per year for the last twenty years. Today it is estimated that one in every eight or nine women in the U.S. will develop breast cancer in their life-time.[21] While there is substantial evidence that endocrine disrupting chemicals including pesticides can cause these disorders,[22] we still have insufficient evidence to directly connect these over-all trends.

The known impacts of endocrine disrupters for women include the disruption of normal sexual differentiation of the fetus, reduced ovarian function (i.e. poor follicular growth, ovulation, corpus litium formation and maintenance), and reduced rates of fertilization, implantation, and pregnancy.[23]

Exposure to organochloride insecticides is suspected of playing an important role in breast cancer. One known mechanism involving organochlorines provokes a change in the natural breakdown of estradiol, the most predominant form of estrogen in women. Normally, estradiol is changed into one of two products: one is benign, the other is not. The deleterious compound binds to certain breast cells and causes continuous cell divisions. Uncontrolled growth of these cells leads to breast cancer. Excessive exposure to organochlorines can significantly increase the ratio of deleterious to benign estradiol by-product. This ratio has become a biological marker of risk for breast cancer.[24] It is estimated that forty percent of all cancers in women are hormonally mediated.[25]

The acute effects of many pesticides are well documented; impacting the liver, kidneys, lungs, skin, eyes, and brain.

Endometriosis, an extremely painful reproductive and immunological disease, is on the rise and currently affects 5 million women in the U.S.[26] It too is on the probable suspect list of diseases caused by endocrine disruption. Additionally, women in Ventura County, California, reported a synchronization of their menstrual cycles with the calendar spraying of malathion in attempts to eradicate the Mediterranean Fruit Fly.[27] While the mechanisms of this are not fully understood it is quite likely related to estrogen mimicking. Another study found that young women are reaching puberty at much earlier ages raising additional troubling questions about the impacts of environmental estrogens.[28]

For men, the known impacts of endocrine disrupting chemicals are reduced sperm production, reproductive system abnormalities and testicular cancer.[29] Additionally, a recent study found a correlation between number of nearby acres sprayed with herbicide and prostate cancer deaths.[30] In males, one gene on the Y chromosome triggers the development of the testis. All of the other distinguishing features of male physiology are developed by the testosterone and androgen[31] which are produced there. Some of the developmental disorders associated with hormone disruption in male newborns are un-descended testicles (cryptorchidism) and abnormal urethreal openings (hypospadias), which have also doubled in the last half-century.[32]

Documented effects of endocrine disrupting chemicals on wild animals include the low male hatching rates and survival in western gulls apparently resulting in same sex nesting discovered among females.[33] Alligators living in Lake Apopka, Florida, contaminated in 1980 with dicofol spilled by the Tower Chemical Company, have continued to exhibit reproductive problems, including underdeveloped penises,[34] long after water sampling has shown the lake to have recovered. We have seen the feminization of rainbow trout, masculinization of marine snails, mosquito fish, grizzly and black bears; and decreased hatching of bald eagle eggs, foster's tern, cardinals, mocking birds, and snapping turtles; and reduced thyroid function of salmon and herring gulls.[35]

An increased threat

A study published in *Science* showed that pesticides may be thousands of times more potent than previously thought.[36] It demonstrated that, when tested alone, each of two particular organochlorine pesticides had to be at concentrations 100,000 times greater than natural estrogen to cause responses in yeast cells reactive to estrogen. Yet the same two organochlorines mixed together only required concentrations between 10 and 100 times more than natural estrogen to induce the same response. Thus, exposure to multiple pesticides may be thousands of times more potent in mimicking estrogen than was previously thought. This study has yet to be reproduced in laboratory setting, but considering the diversity of pesticides found in our environment (a recent study found thirty percent of a single fruit alone, apples, contain at least three different pesticide residues),[37] the increased potency of combined pesticides raises many questions. Does this mean that current tolerance levels set for individual pesticide residues allowed in our food are actually far above dangerous limits when combined? What are the implications for the unborn, children, and adolescents? In light of these findings, how should pesticide use be assessed? How should new chemicals be evaluated? And, what are the implications for future pesticide policy formulation?

The significance of the additive nature of pesticides is evident in light of the extensive use and accumulation of pesticides in both the environment and living organisms. Since their widespread use began after the Second World War, world pesticide use has increased dramatically. In 1993, approximately 4.5 billion pounds of "conventional pesticide active ingredients" used for agricultural purposes were applied throughout the world; 24% of those pesticides or over 1 billion pounds were used in the U.S. equivalent to 4.1 pounds per person. In 1995, California alone applied over 210 million pounds of active ingredient,[38] or an alarming 6.6 pounds per person. California has reported a 10% average annual increase in pesticide use[39] over the last five years, consuming almost five percent of global use.[40]

Exposure to organochloride insecticides is suspected of playing an important role in breast cancer.

Pesticide exposure is nearly impossible to estimate on an individual or per capita basis because there are so many distinct exposure pathways. Pesticides are in our food, water, and air. They are now a nearly universal feature of our environment found in every ecosystem in the world, and are used not only in food production and commercial forestry, but also in our homes, schools, public parks, and work places. Pesticides are a pervasive part of our environment—virtually impossible to avoid.

Even as we are now discovering that pesticides pose a much greater threat to society than ever before suspected, the U.S. government is undermining already limited regulations. August 3, 1996, marked a new era for pesticide regulation roll back in the U.S., as President Bill Clinton signed into law the Food Quality Protection Act, dramatically changing the way we regulate the dangers of pesticides in our food. This new law, which President Clinton preferred to call the "Peace of Mind Act," cleverly eliminated the Delaney clause of the Federal Food, Drug, and Cosmetic Act which prohibited the existence of carcinogenic residues in all processed foods. As industry cheers "Ding-dong Delaney's dead,"[41] known carcinogens and other toxic chemicals are being allowed into our food supply—but only in quantities which are determined "safe" by the EPA. In other words, policy makers moved by major pesticide industry lobby groups such as the American Crop Protection Association (ACPA), have lowered our food safety standard from one of banning known carcinogens, to just "managing" the risk of having them in our food.

Pesticides are a pervasive part of our environment—virtually impossible to avoid.

In light of endocrine disruption, this new reliance on tolerance levels and risk management poses many problems for consumers. First and foremost, a high proportion of pesticides registered for use have never had full toxicological studies and risk assessments performed on them. This is due to a lack of funding and political will on the part of state and federal agencies. Secondly, the only pesticides tested for endocrine disruption are those that are related to very specific events linking them to a rare health or environmental impact, thus bringing them under suspicion. There is no standardized screening protocol or series of tests for endocrine disruption that all pesticides must pass to get registered.[42] Third, there are specific windows of vulnerability to specific endocrine disrupters such that we have different susceptibility at different ages.[43] Thus each test must be done on the different stages of human development starting in the first trimester of pregnancy and continuing through adolescence and adulthood creating different tolerances for different stages of development. Fourth, pesticides react with the endocrine system in unpredictable ways, some are estrogen mimickers at low doses and estrogen blockers at high doses.[44] Finally, tolerance levels based on single chemicals do not take into account the synergistic or additive effects of two or more endocrine disrupters or the cumulative effects of pesticides that have the same biochemical impacts on our bodies.[45]

The Environmental Protection Agency has created the Endocrine Disrupter Screening and Testing Advisory Committee (EDSTAC) to try to solve some of these issues. The work groups which have been established include members of the chemical industry, governmental agencies, university researchers, and public interest groups. The quantity of research that would be required to begin to set new tolerance levels combined with the poor regulatory and enforcement track records of our federal and state agencies bring this whole approach into question.

One of the most prominent examples of the lack of control by the Food and Drug Administration (FDA) occurred when illegal residues of chlorpyrifos, an organophosphate insecticide, were detected in Cheerios brand breakfast cereal. By the time it was discovered, over one year's worth of contaminated Cheerios had already been sold and consumed, and the FDA could not recall boxes already in commerce without declaring a public health emergency. Furthermore, General Mills sold the remaining 18 million bushels of contaminated oats as animal feed[46] which, if used for either meat or dairy production, would still reach consumers through accumulation in the food chain. This contamination of our food supply is a direct reflection of the broader failure of the FDA's regulatory power.

Reducing the dangers

If so many illegal residues already slip through the system, perhaps the FDA and EPA are not the answer. We must ask the more fundamental question: "Is lowering tolerance levels and increasing pesticide monitoring an appropriate strategy to guarantee a safe and secure food supply?"

The fact that we have residues of hundreds of industrial and agricultural chemicals in our bodies is a direct physical invasion. A chemical that presents serious health risks, should simply be banned from use. Under such a policy, research would be focused on detecting those chemicals which cause serious health problems and then ban them. This would reduce the whole research task of developing tolerance levels and eliminate the risk rather than attempting to manage it. Effective alternatives currently exist for most pesticides,[47] and the social costs of continuing their use may out-weigh the short-term economic gains they provide to the chemical and food companies.

Effective alternatives currently exist for most pesticides.

Although organic food is more expensive than that grown with pesticides, the external costs of pesticides are not included in the price of commercially grown food. It has been very roughly estimated that in the U.S. a direct investment of $4 billion in pesticides saves about $16 billion in crop losses but causes an estimated $8 billion in externalized environmental and health costs. Five billion of that is paid for by society and not by chemical companies or direct users.[48] Buying organic food from local farms not only enhances our own health and that of future generations, but it also benefits us as it decreases pollution, supports local, small scale farmers and makes farming itself more sustainable in the long run.

Possible solutions

• Reduce or eliminate the use of pesticides in your local community. Eliminate pesticides from your home and garden. Work with local businesses and government agencies to reduce use in your work place, schools and universities, public buildings, and parks and recreational facilities.

Work with local farmers to alter the farming practices in the region. Support those farms which use alternative practices.

• Demand that the government ban the use of dangerous and unnecessary endocrine disrupting chemicals. Get involved in the EDSTAC process (see below).

• Buy organic food. Organic food can be found in supermarkets, green stores, and health food stores.

• Join a Community Supported Agriculture (CSA) Farm. As a member you buy shares of a farmer's crop, and may also assist with some aspect of the farm operation in exchange for fresh produce. For more information contact CSA of North America at (413) 528-4374 or call Food First for a directory of Bay Area CSAs at (510) 645-4400.

• Shop at Farmers Markets. Many farmers markets focus primarily on organic produce. To locate a local farmers market call your state Department of Agriculture.

• Join Food Buying Cooperatives. To create or join a food co-op near you, contact the National Cooperative Business Association at (202) 638-6222 or write Co-op Directory Services, 919 21st Ave. So., Minneapolis, MN 55404.

• Cut back on meat and dairy consumption because pesticides accumulate in animal fat and milk. If possible, buy organic dairy products.

• Exercise. It decreases the deleterious by-product of estradiol metabolism, mobilizes fat stores so that pesticides do not accumulate in your body.

• For more information on Endocrine Disruptor Screening and Testing Advisory Committee (EDSTAC) visit their world wide web page at http://www.epa.gov/opptintr/opptendo/index.htm, or get on their Public Fax/Mailing List by calling (970) 262-6278.

Notes

1. Carson, Rachel. Silent Spring. Houghton Mifflin Co., Boston. 1962.

2. Colborn T, D Dumanoski, and J.P. Myers. Our Stolen Future. Are we threatening our fertility, intelligence, and survival?—a science detective story. Penguin Books, New York. 1996.

3. The U.S. EPA and the National Institute for Health and Human Services have at least three separate bodies each working on this issue. The U.S. Dept. of the Interior, National Research Council and the National Academy of Science are also formulating research and policy agendas. England has six government offices working on this issue, and the European Union held a workshop Dec. 2–4, 1996 to develop their research agenda. The OECD held a workshop on harmonization issues covering endocrine disruption in Solna, Sweden January 22–24, 1996. Also see Kavlock et al. "Research Needs for the Assessment of Health and Environmental Effects of Endocrine Disrupters: A report of the U.S. EPA-sponsored workshop." Environmental Health Perspectives 104 (Suppl 4): 715–740, 1996.; and Ankley GT, RD Johnson, G Toth, LC Folmar, NE Detenbeck, and SP Bradbury. "Development of a research strategy for assessing the ecological risk of endocrine disrupters." Environmental Toxicology, 1996.

4. Carson, R 1962 op. cit.

5. Colborn, T et al. 1996 op. cit.

6. ibid.

7. Crisp, TM, ED Clegg, RL Cooper. Special Report on Environmental Endocrine Disruption: An Effect Assessment and Analysis. Risk Assessment Forum, Office of Water, U.S. EPA. Washington, DC. 1997. Doc. # EPA/630/R-96/012.

8. Arnold SF, DM Klotz, BM Collins, PM Vonier, LJ Guillette, JA McLachlan. "Synergistic activation of estrogen receptor with combinations of environmental chemicals." Science 272:1489–1492, 1996.

9. DPR. Pesticide Use Reports for 1995. Department of Pesticide Regulation Cal EPA, Sacramento, CA. 1996.

10. The BMA Guide to Pesticides, Chemicals, and Health. London : Published on behalf of the British Medical Association, by Edward Arnold, 1992.

11. The Effects of pesticides on human health: proceedings of a workshop, May 9–11, 1988, Keystone, Colorado. Task Force of Environmental Cancer and Heart and Lung Disease; editor Scott R. Baker. Princeton : Princeton Scientific Pub. Co., 1990.; and Hayes, W. Handbook of Pesticide Toxicology. Academic Press. 1991.

12. Norstrom R, D Hallett, and R Sonstegard. "Coho Salmon (Oncorhynchus kisutch) and Herring Gulls (Larus arentatus) as Indicators of Organochlorine Contamination in Lake Ontario," Journal of the Fisheries Research Board of Canada 35(11): 1401–1409, 1978; and Fox G. "What Have Biomarkers Told Us About the Effects of Contaminants on the Health of Fish-Eating Birds of the Great Lakes? The Theory and a Literature Review", Journal of Great Lakes Research 19(4): 722–36, 1993.

13. Jensen A, and Slorach S, Chemical Contaminants in Human Milk, CRC Press, 1991; and Thomas K, and T Colborn, "Organoclorine Endocrine Disrupters in Human Tissue", in Chemically Induced Alterations in Sexual and Functional Development: The Wildlife-Human Connection, T. Colborn and C. Clement eds. Princeton Scientific Publishing, 1992, pp 365–94.

14. Besedovsky HO, A Del Rey. "Immune-neuro-endocrine interactions: facts and hypotheses". Endocrine Review 17:64–102, 1996. ; Dussault JH, and Ruel J. "Thyroid hormones and brain development" Annual Review of Physiology 49:321–334, 1987.; and Fuchs BA, and VM Saunders. "The role of brain-immune system interactions in immunotoxicology" Critical Review of Toxicology 24:151–176, 1994.

15. Crisp et al. 1997 op. cit.

16. Colborn et al. 1996 op.cit.; and Colborn T, FS vom Saal, AM Soto. "Developmental Effects of Endocrine Disrupting Chemicals in Wildlife and Humans", Environmental Health Perspectives, 101:378–384, 1993.

17. Bitman J and HC Cecil. "Estrogenic activity of DDT analogs and polychlorinated biphenyls" Journal of Agricultural and Food Chemistry, 18:1108–1112, 1970. Rolland R, M Gilbertson, T Colborn. "Environmentally induced alterations in development: A focus on wildlife". Environmental Health Perspectives 103 (Suppl 4):1–106, 1995.; Birnbaum LS. "Endocrine effects of prenatal exposure to PCBs, dioxins, and other xenobiotics; implications for policy and future research". Environmental Health Perspectives 102:676–679, 1994.; Colborn T, Clement C, eds. "Chemically Induced Alterations in Sexual and Functional Development:

The Wildlife/Human Connection. Princeton Scientific Publishing Co. Inc, Princeton, NJ, 1992, 403.; Kelce WR, CR Stone, SC Laws, LE Gray Jr, JA Kemppainen, EM Wilson. "Persistent DDT metabolite p,p'-DDE is a potent androgen receptor antagonist." Nature 375:581–585, 1995b.; and Sharpe RM and NE Skakkebaek. "Are oestrogens involved in falling sperm counts and disorders of the male reproductive tract?" Lancet 341:1392–1395, 1993.

18. Carlsen E, A Giwercman, N Keiding, NE Skakkebaek. "Evidence for decreasing quality of semen during past 50 years". Br Med J 305:609–613, 1992. and Carlsen E, A Giwercman, N Keiding, NE Skakkebaek. "Declining semen quality and increased incidence of testicular cancer: Is there a common cause?" Environmental Health Perspectives, 193 (supplement 7): 137–139, 1995.

19. Potosky Al, BA Miller, PC Albertsen, BS Kramer. "The role of increasing detection in the rising incidence of prostate cancer." JAMA 273:548–552, 1995.

20. Toppari J, JC Larsen, P Christiansen, A Giwercman, and others. Male Reproductive Health and Environmental Chemicals with Estrogenic Effects. Miljoprojekt nr. 290. Report of the Ministry of Environment and Energy, Danish Environmental Protection Agency, Kobenhavn, Denmark, 1995.

21. Silverberg E, and JA Lubera. "Cancer statistic", 1988. CA Cancer J Clin 38:5–22, 1988. and Miller BA, EJ Feuer, BF Hankey. "The significance of the rising incidence of breast cancer in the U.S." In: Important Advance in Oncology 1994, DeVita VT Jr, S Hellman, SA Rosenberg eds., J B Lippincott Company, Philadelphia, PA, 1994.

22. Davis DL, HL Bradlow, M Wolff, T Woodruff, and others, "Medical Hypothesis: xenoestrogens as preventable causes of breast cancer" Environmental Health Perspectives 101: 372–377, 1993.; Skakkebaek NE, JG Berthelsen, A Giwercman, J Muller. "Carcinoma-in-situ of the testis: possible origin from gonocytes and precurser of all types of germ cell tumours except spermatocytoma" International Journal Andrololology 10:19–28,1987.; Slattery ML, and DW West. "Smoking, alcohol, coffee, tea, caffeine, and theobromine: risk of prostate cancer in Utah (United States)". Cancer Causes Control 4:559–563, 1993.

23. Crisp et al. 1997 op. cit.

24. Bradlow HL; DL Davis; G LIN; D Sepkovik; and others. "Effects of Pesticides on the Ratio of 16-Alpha/2-Hydroxyesterone—A Biological Marker of Breast Cancer Risk." Environmental Health Perspectives, 1995 Oct, V103 S7:147–150.

25. Davis et al. 1993 op. cit.

26. Crisp et al. 1997 op. cit.

27. Personal communication, Deborah Bectal, XI Annual California Pesticide Organizing Conference. May 3–4 Berkeley, 1997.

28. Herman-Giddens ME; EJ Slora, RC Wasserman, CJ Bourdony, and others. "Secondary sexual characteristics and menses in young girls seen in office practice: A study from the pediatric research in office settings network". Pediatrics, 1997 April, V99 N4:505–512.

29. Crisp et al. 1997 op. cit.

30. Morrison H, D Savitz, R Semenciw, B Hulka, and others. Farming and prostate cancer mortality. American Journal of Epidemiology 137:270–280, 1993.

31. a male hormone that also exists in women at low levels

32. Carlsen et al. 1995 op. cit.

33. Fry M. "Reproductive effects in birds exposed to pesticides and industrial chemicals". Environmental Health Perspectives 103(Suppl 7):165–171, 1995; and Fry DM, CK Toone, SM Speich, RJ Peard. "Sex ratio skew and breeding patterns of gulls: demographic and toxicological considerations". Study of Avian Biology 10:26–43, 1987.

34. Guillette LJ Jr, DB Pickford, DA Crain, AA Rooney, HF Percival. "Reduction in penis size and plasma testosterone concentrations in juvenile alligators living in a contaminated environment". General and Comparative Endocrinology 101:32–34, 1996.

35. Crisp et al. 1997 op. cit.

36. Arnold, et al. 1996 op. cit.

37. Elderkin, S. Forbidden Fruit: illegal pesticides in the U.S. food supply. Washington, DC: Environmental Working Group, 1995.

38. DPR 1995 op. cit.

39. ibid.

40. ibid.

41. "Industry Rejoices as DC Enviros Fumble Again". Food and Water Journal, Winter 1997 p. 43.

42. Crisp et al. 1997 op. cit.

43. ibid.

44. Personal communication, Dr. Gina Solomon, Keynote Presentation, XI Annual California Pesticide Organizing Conference. May 3–4 Berkeley, 1997.

45. Arnold et al. 1996 op. cit.

46. Elderkin, S. 1995 op. cit.

47. Benbrook C, E Groth, JM Halloran, MK Hansen, and S Marquardt. Pest Management at the Crossroads. Consumers Union, New York. 1996; EPA, Alternatives to Methyl Bromide Vol. I & II. Environmental Protection Agency, Stratospheric Ozone Protection. Office of Air and Radiation, 1996.; Fox SJ. Database of alternatives to targeted pesticides. University of California Division of Agriculture Statewide IPM Project, University of California, Davis, 1991; and Gips, Terry. Breaking the pesticide habit: alternatives to 12 hazardous pesticides. International Alliance for Sustainable Agriculture, Minn. 1987.

48. Pimintel, D et al. "Environmental and economic costs of pesticides" Bioscience 42(10), 750–760.

7

Irradiation Helps Improve Food Safety

P.J. Skerrett

P.J. Skerrett is a freelance writer who has co-authored books on health and the environment.

Irradiation, the use of gamma rays, x-rays, or electron beams to kill harmful organisms in meat, produce, grains, and spices, is an effective way of improving the safety of America's food supply. Despite the fact that food irradiation is beneficial and does not pose health risks, it has yet to become widely used. The high costs of irradiation are one reason, but the main impediment to its use are environmental organizations, such as Food and Water, which use scare tactics and inaccurate arguments in an effort to frighten and intimidate the public and corporations. However, consumers have responded favorably to irradiated food when it has been commercially available, which suggests that the method may become more widespread.

In food we trust. That motto guides us as much as the one that graces our currency. We take for granted the food we buy in grocery stores or eat in restaurants, trusting implicitly that it will satisfy our hunger, build strong bodies 12 ways, and keep us healthy.

That trust may be a bit misplaced. Nearly 200 people in the United States, most of them children or elderly, die each week from illnesses they contract from food. Estimates from the Centers for Disease Control and Prevention in Washington, D.C., suggest that 6 to 33 million people are stricken with food-borne diseases each year. Major outbreaks are grabbing headlines with greater frequency—consider the Hudson Foods recall of 25 million pounds of bacteria-tainted beef, contaminated Jack-in-the-Box hamburgers, Odwalla apple juice, and Guatemalan raspberries—while many minor ones go unreported.

In spring 1997, President Bill Clinton gave voice to growing concern by public-health officials over our food supply by calling for "new steps using cutting-edge technology to keep our food safe." One of the technologies that Clinton singles out in his proposed $43 million National Food Safety Initiative is food irradiation, a process that has long been lauded by food-safety experts even as it languishes in the backwaters of research and development. "If the president's program takes hold, food irradiation could get the political push it needs," says James Tillotson, director of the Food Policy Institute at Tufts University.

"The benefits of food irradiation are overwhelming," says Richard Lechowich, director of the National Center for Food Safety and Technology at the Illinois Institute of Technology. High-energy radiation kills critters that live in or on food, including the deadly E. coli O157:H7 bacterium and the salmonella and campylobacter species of bacteria found in most uncooked chicken and turkey. "Widespread irradiation of poultry alone in this country could prevent thousands of illnesses and hundreds of deaths every year," concurs Douglas Archer, former deputy director of the Center for Food Safety and Applied Nutrition at the U.S. Food and Drug Administration (FDA).

It does not appear that irradiated food causes cancer.

A major benefit of irradiation is that it can occur after food is packaged and sealed to kill any organisms that may have contaminated the food between production line and plate. "We don't live in a perfect world where we always detect E. coli on a processing line, and where everyone washes their hands and cutting boards and cooks meat and poultry to the proper temperature," says Christine Bruhn, director of the Center for Consumer Research at the University of California at Davis. Food irradiation is like an air bag in a car, she says. Both offer an extra measure of safety in case of carelessness or accident.

More than 40 countries share this view, having authorized irradiation for everything from apples in China and frog legs in France to rice in Mexico, raw pork sausages in Thailand, and wheat in Canada. Irradiation has been endorsed not only by the U.N. World Health Organization and the Food and Agriculture Organization, but also by the U.S. Food and Drug Administration, the American Medical Association, and the American Public Health Association, among others. The process can legally be used in the United States for killing insects in grains, flour, fruits, and vegetables; for preventing stored potatoes, onions, and garlic from sprouting; and for killing microbes, insects, and parasites in spices, pork, and poultry.

But despite such wide-ranging approval, actual use of irradiation in the United States has been limited. Astronauts have eaten irradiated food ever since the Apollo 17 moon shot in 1972, when they carried sandwiches made from irradiated ham, cheese, and bread. Space shuttle crews dine on radiation-treated food, and it will almost certainly show up on space station menus. Some hospitals and nursing homes serve irradiated chicken to people with weakened immune systems, including AIDS patients, burn victims, people undergoing chemotherapy, and patients who have just had a bone marrow or organ transplant. And a few independent grocers carry irradiated produce and poultry. But the vast majority of companies that grow, process, or sell food shy away from this technology.

Why? The food industry has been reluctant partly because of public fear of radiation. In fact, a savvy organization of activists known as Food and Water claims it has held food processors in check simply by threatening to expose any company that dares use the technique. But that may change. Advocates contend that such fears of irradiated food are not only groundless but, with each news report of contaminated food, fading quickly as consumers consider the alternative of ignoring this safeguard. The issue now, they say, is whether the technology is ready for commercial use and can work at reasonable cost.

Although food irradiation is often referred to as a cutting-edge technology, its beginnings stretch back nearly a century. A few years after radiation was discovered by French physicist Antoine-Henri Becquerel in 1896, Samuel Prescott, professor of biology at the Massachusetts Institute of Technology (MIT), showed that gamma rays from radium destroyed bacteria in food and proposed using radiation to preserve meat, fruit, vegetables, grains, and other foodstuffs. In the 1920s and 1930s, the United States and France awarded patents for radiation-based methods of killing parasites in pork and bacteria in canned food. Some 25 years of research at MIT and U.S. Army research facilities—from 1943 to 1968—further demonstrated its potential for treating and preserving food.

This high-tech cousin of canning, freezing, and fumigating relies on a simple principle that children of the atomic age know by heart: radiation kills, or at least alters, living cells. When gamma rays or other types of ionizing radiation zip through a cell, they knock some electrons out of their orbits, breaking chemical bonds and leaving behind a trail of ions and free radicals—atoms or molecules with an unpaired electron. These highly reactive substances crash into each other and into their nonirradiated neighbors, creating some new compounds and reforming many that had originally been there.

When a cell is exposed to high enough doses of radiation, the maelstrom of chemical reactions inside an irradiated cell inactivates key enzymes, irreparably damages the cell's genetic instructions, and can disrupt its protective outer membrane. The cell either stops growing and fails to reproduce or dies outright. Either of these outcomes destroys organisms that are natural or introduced contaminants of food or other products or prevents them from multiplying.

Critics of irradiation

Though some foods such as cucumbers, grapes, and some tomatoes turn mushy when radiation breaks cell walls and release enzymes that digest the food and speed up rotting, many others including strawberries, apples, onions, mushrooms, pork, poultry, red meat, and seafood emerge from irradiation intact and edible. But while these foods can legally be irradiated, virtually none of them are.

The problem isn't necessarily radiation itself, because people don't seem to mind that it is used to sterilize half of all sutures, syringes, intravenous lines, and other medical supplies, as well as billions of dollars worth of consumer goods ranging from plastic wrap and milk cartons to tampons and contact lenses. What poses concerns is the juxtaposition of food and irradiation. "Food is a very emotional thing," says Tillotson of Tufts. "We don't want scientists or anyone else mucking around with it, especially not with something that most people link with the atomic bomb."

The activists at Food and Water of Walden, Vermont, effectively manipulate this potential reaction. This grassroots group, founded in 1984 to fight hunger, now spends its time fighting food irradiation, genetic engineering, and other technologies used to grow and process food, while advocating a smaller-is-better, back-to-the-land approach.

A willing David to the food industry's Goliath, Food and Water has almost singlehandedly blocked the commercialization of food irradiation. Larger organizations such as Ralph Nader's Public Citizen weigh in on the matter from time to time—"Whenever we need a quote from the big boys," boasts Food and Water's executive director, Michael Colby—but no longer actively campaign against food irradiation because, they say, Food and Water is carrying the ball.

Food and Water charges that irradiation seriously depletes the nutritional value of food, introduces carcinogens, and is essentially a cover-up that allows corporations to sell previously contaminated items. But these charges don't stand up to the evidence or aren't as dire as Food and Water alleges.

It is true that irradiation can alter the nutritional content of food. While no carbohydrates, protein, fats, or minerals are lost, as much as 10 percent of vitamins A, B-1 (thiamine), E, and K can disappear at FDA-approved sterilization doses. But it's also true that similar vitamin losses occur when fresh fruits and vegetables are canned or even when they sit in cold storage.

Irradiation is safe

More important, it does not appear that irradiated food causes cancer. First of all, when a hunk of hamburger is zapped with radiation it does not become radioactive, just as you don't start glowing after an x-ray. At the energy levels used for food, ionizing radiation doesn't have the oomph to knock a neutron away from an atom's nucleus or force an atom to fission. Instead, the radiation leaves behind traces of radiolytic compounds—which merely means broken (lysis) by radiant energy (radio)—that are identical to compounds that naturally occur in the foods we eat every day.

Cancer researcher George Tritsch, now retired from the Roswell Park Cancer Institute in Buffalo, New York, and an adviser to Food and Water, points out that some of these radiolytic products are known carcinogens, such as benzene and formaldehyde, and worries that adding more of these products, though measured in parts per billion, will raise cancer rates. This would be a formidable argument if it weren't for the fact that many foods naturally contain much higher levels of these and other cancer-causing agents, says Donald Thayer, research leader for food safety at the U.S. Department of Agriculture's Eastern Regional Research Center. Eggs, for example, contain 100 times more benzene than the highest levels found in food exposed to the maximum doses of sterilizing radiation.

Colby also argues that irradiation may create radiolytic compounds never before identified in food, some of which might cause cancer or other health problems. But he is unable to cite any examples. And, according to Thayer, "in more than 40 years of looking, no one has yet found in foods any compounds unique to the radiation process."

Nor have animal tests turned up any cause for concern. Under the direction of Edward Josephson, professor emeritus of food and nutrition at the University of Rhode Island, researchers at the U.S. Army's Natick (Mass.) laboratories fed irradiated chicken, wheat, oranges, and other foods to four generations of mice, three generations of beagles, and thousands of rats, guinea pigs, and monkeys from the late 1950s to the early 1960s. Even though the radiation doses were 10 to 20 times higher than necessary, he says, the animals eating irradiated foods suffered no more cancer or inherited diseases than animals eating either canned or frozen nonirradiated food.

An inadvertent test of irradiated foods comes from the Paterson Institute for Cancer Research in Manchester, England. Since 1987, several thousand mice with impaired immune systems have eaten nothing but radiation-sterilized food. After more than 60 generations, these mice show no more cancers or other diseases than similar mice fed heat-sterilized food.

Finally, the relatively few human studies that have been conducted also suggest that eating irradiated food is safe. In the early 1980s, more than 400 volunteers ate irradiated food for 7 to 15 weeks as part of eight separate studies in China. The volunteers showed no more chromosomal abnormalities—an early warning sign of cancer-causing activity—than those who ate nonirradiated food.

Opponents of food irradiation argue that critical tests remain to be done before anyone can say the process is absolutely without risk. Colby argues for standard toxicology tests that would involve irradiating an apple, say, then extracting any radiolytic products that form and feeding those compounds to lab animals at doses hundreds of times higher than that found in irradiated food.

But Josephson, for one, thinks that this exercise is unnecessary. "Why should we feed animals huge doses of these compounds," he says, "when years of animal-feeding studies have already shown that the small amounts that occur in irradiated food don't cause any health or reproductive problems?"

The relatively few human studies that have been conducted . . . suggest that eating irradiated food is safe.

Food and Water adviser Donald Louria, chair of preventive medicine and community health at the University of Medicine and Dentistry of New Jersey, would go one step further than Colby. He says government or industry should fund a study in which volunteers of different ages, races, and socioeconomic backgrounds eat irradiated foods under controlled conditions, and then undergo tests to see if they have higher-than-normal levels of cells with chromosomal abnormalities.

On that score, however, the FDA apparently disagrees. Back in 1958, Congress defined irradiation as an additive rather than a process, even though radiation generates the same sorts of chemical byproducts in food as other processes used to preserve and protect food, including freeze drying, frying, sun drying, and canning. And FDA regulations don't require human studies for food additives, especially when the compounds added are identical to those already found in food, says George Pauli, the FDA's senior food irradiation scientist.

Ironically, neither Food and Water nor any other group is calling for the FDA to reclassify or restudy other techniques that produce the same byproducts. In fact, until the U.S. Army animal experiments, canned food had never been rigorously tested to see if it caused cancer. "People in the canning industry were holding their breath," recalls Josephson, "hoping we weren't going to find that canned food caused problems compared with irradiated food."

Obstacles to irradiation

Food and Water's arguments may be shaky, but its public-relations acumen is rock solid, and highly effective. The organization deftly links people's worst fears about radiation to food. For example, one classic Food and Water advertisement shows a mushroom cloud erupting from a freshly cooked hamburger. The message reads: "The Department of Energy has a solution to the problem of radioactive waste. You're going to eat it."

The organization knows how to pressure executives who fear any sort of public controversy. When Food and Water learned that a representative from Hormel Foods attended a 1996 symposium on the benefits of food irradiation, it demanded to know the company's official policy on this technology.

When letters failed, Food and Water sought help from its constituents, which Colby claims total some 100,000, though a recent *Wall Street Journal* article places that figure considerably lower, at around 3,500. Colby asked members of Food and Water's grassroots network to let Hormel know how they felt about irradiation, and supplied preprinted postcards and a listing of Hormel's toll-free phone number.

The organization also ran a full-page ad showing a glowing can of irradiated Spam—one of Hormel's most widely recognized products—in the company's hometown newspaper on the day of its annual stockholder meeting and threatened Hormel officials that it would run the ads nationwide. Copies were sent to 18,000 food-industry executives. Two weeks later, Hormel issued a statement saying that it does not irradiate food. Food and Water suspended the campaign but threatened to resurrect it if Hormel "ever considers using food irradiation in the future."

Colby calls this approach "corporate education" and grassroots activism. Others see it differently. "The organization is shaping the debate and food policy through public fear mongering and scare tactics," says UC Davis's Bruhn.

Food and Water's anti-irradiation campaign may be the most public obstacle to wider use of food irradiation, but it isn't the only one. "The real barrier is economics and the bottom line," says Martin Stein, president of GrayStar, which is designing a food irradiator that can be installed in existing food-processing plants. In fact, a quick review of the methods the food industry could employ to generate ionizing radiation—using gamma rays from radioactive cobalt-60 or cesium-137, and electron beams or x-rays from linear accelerators—shows that the options have shortcomings that diminish their cost effectiveness, while improved models are still on the drawing board.

Methods of irradiation

• *GAMMA RAYS:* Anyone interested in irradiating food today would probably turn to a cobalt-60-based system like the one in Mulberry, Florida, the first commercial facility dedicated to irradiating food. The heart of the plant, established in 1991, is a shiny rack of 400 gamma-ray-emitting cobalt-60 "pencils," each 18 inches long and the diameter of a fat crayon, housed in a chamber surrounded by a concrete wall 6 feet thick. When not in use, the rack is submerged in a 15-foot-deep pool of cooled water that absorbs and neutralizes the gamma rays. At the push of a button, hydraulic arms lift the cobalt rack out of its protective pool and tall metal boxes packed with food slide into the irradiation chamber on an overhead monorail. The boxes follow a zig-zag pattern around the radioactive rack so gamma rays can reach all sides. Treatment times vary—fresh strawberries pass through in 5 to 8 minutes, frozen chicken takes as long as 20 minutes.

Gamma rays from cobalt-60 can penetrate full boxes of fresh or frozen food. But food must be removed from standard shipping pallets, stacked into metal irradiation boxes, and then returned to the pallets when they emerge from the chamber—all extra labor that increases costs.

A new irradiator now under development by GrayStar promises to address this concern by accepting food loaded onto standard pallets, something "everyone in the food industry says is an absolute must," says Stein. The unit will generate gamma rays using cesium-137, which GrayStar would chemically separate from high-level nuclear waste now stored at several power plants around the country.

The prototype machine—which measures 10 feet wide, 8 feet long, and 28 feet high, 12 of which are underground—is designed to be installed along a meat-packing or food-processing line. After a standard pallet of packaged food rolls into the irradiation chamber, which is constructed from 16-inch steel walls, the operator will seal the doors and instruct a computer to raise the rectangular array of cesium-containing rods from underground for a programmed length of time. Stein is optimistic that the unit will prove attractive to food processors and packers who may be more willing to invest in small, in-house irradiators than build, or contract with, a large central plant to which it must ship food. A working prototype of the compact unit, he says, is still a year away.

• *ELECTRON BEAMS AND X-RAYS:* Linear accelerators can generate ionizing radiation for food processing in the form of electron beams. Like a television set, these devices produce electrons from a heated filament sitting inside a vacuum tube. Magnetic fields accelerate the electrons through the tube until they reach energies as high as 10 million electron volts. At the end of the tube, meat or other food is irradiated as it slides by on a conveyor belt. Turn off the juice and the radiation disappears. A linear accelerator delivers more radiation per second than gamma rays; so it may work more quickly than a cobalt- or cesium-based machine.

"The downside is that electrons don't penetrate more than an inch and a half. Thus electron beams would not be able to handle such items as boxes of fruit or sides of beef. However, says Dennis Olson, a professor of food science at Iowa State University who has been testing this method, "you could handle a product up to about three inches thick, something like hamburger or chicken breasts, if you irradiate from both sides." Electron-beam units for such thin food products could move from the lab to the factory within a year or two at today's pace of development, according to Spencer Stevens, president of Omaha-based APA, Inc., an engineering and consulting firm for the food and meat industry.

Olson and others are also exploring the use of x-rays for irradiating food. While it takes even more energy to make x-rays than it does to generate electron beams, thus lowering the efficiency of the process, x-rays have dramatically better penetrating power and could be used on stacked boxes of fresh or frozen food or on slabs of meat.

Consumer response to irradiation

Economics will play a large role in determining which of these approaches, if any, will ever be widely used in food processing. As commodities go, food is cheap, so even slight increases in processing costs can have a big impact on what consumers pay for certain items. Thus, says Stevens, radiation processing can't cost more than a few cents a pound, a figure that in-house irradiators could soon meet.

But the biggest unknown, of course, is whether consumers will buy irradiated food, even if producers can provide it at an affordable price. A series of surveys from the University of California at Davis, the University of Georgia, and Indiana University suggest the public is ready. "When you ask people if they would ever buy irradiated food, 50 to 60 percent say they would," says UC Davis's Bruhn. "When you mention that irradiation can keep food fresh longer and kill bacteria, the percentage rises to 80."

In-store tests and actual sales from a few independent grocery and produce stores offer real-world evidence that consumers might follow through on what they say. For example, Olson and his colleagues at Iowa State University sold irradiated chicken at a grocery store in Manhattan, Kansas. Radiation-treated chicken—clearly labeled with a green symbol called a radura that must legally appear on all irradiated food—was displayed next to the traditionally processed store brand. Whichever one was cheaper sold better. Sales split down the middle when both carried the same price tag. Even when the irradiated chicken cost almost 25 cents a pound more, it still accounted for 20 percent of sales, says Olson.

Carrot Top, a produce store in north-suburban Chicago, also has had success selling irradiated food. Owner Jim Corrigan first introduced irradiated strawberries in 1992 with a two-for-one sale, expecting his customers to buy a box of irradiated strawberries and one of nonirradiated strawberries for comparison. Instead, the berries treated with radiation, which killed the molds normally growing on the fruit, outsold untreated berries ten-to-one because they looked better and lasted far longer. Carrot Top has since expanded its irradiated line to include Vidalia onions, blueberries, chicken, exotic Hawaiian fruits, and any other irradiated foods that are available. "I would carry irradiated hamburger today if it were available, since my customers ask me for it," says Corrigan.

None of the country's major food companies will publicly acknowledge even a remote interest in food irradiation, yet several developments could push the food industry to adopt irradiation. First, some "traditional" methods for ridding food of pests are under close scrutiny. Methyl bromide, used to fumigate cereal grains, dried fruits and nuts, and fresh fruits and vegetables is scheduled to be banned in the United States as of January 1, 2001. Not only is it toxic to workers—the Environmental Protection Agency classifies it as a Category I acute toxin, the most deadly kind—it also is 50 times more destructive to the ozone layer than chlorine atoms from chlorofluorocarbons. Radiation could offer a reasonable alternative.

Ionizing radiation can also replace ethylene oxide, another widely used toxic fumigant. Radiation kills bacteria and insects more efficiently than the ethylene oxide, says Thomas Mates, general manager of Steri-Genics, a California company that owns and operates several medical irradiators. What's more, irradiation doesn't leave behind any residue, and doesn't require any moisture, which can remove some of the volatile chemicals that give spices their smell and taste. SteriGenics recently introduced a line of radiation-treated spices called Purely by Choice.

The changing nature of our food supply may also spur wider use of irradiation. Once upon a time Americans got their food from local growers and neighborhood markets. Today much of our food comes from afar— from across the country and increasingly, from developing countries. Few of us would eat fruits and vegetables in many of these countries without washing and peeling them. Yet when they are imported and sold in a U.S. store, that concern seems to disappear. "One does not need to leave home to contract traveler's diarrhea caused by an exotic agent," according to an editorial in the *New England Journal of Medicine* by Michael Osterholm, head of the Minnesota Department of Health. Food irradiation, he contends, "provides the greatest likelihood of substantially reducing bacterial and parasitic causes of food-borne disease associated with numerous foods, including fresh fruits and vegetables."

---

*The changing nature of our food supply may . . .
spur wider use of irradiation.*

Irradiation may get a huge political boost, not to mention funding for further research and development, from the Clinton Administration's food-safety initiative, which is just beginning to wend its way through Congress. Whatever the outcome of the plan, however, the most powerful stimulus for wider use of irradiation is likely to be the ever-larger settlements awarded to people who become sick from eating contaminated food. [In October 1998, Congress allocated $79 million to the initiative.]

A generation ago, individuals felt responsible for the safety of their own food, says Christine Bruhn from UC Davis. Now people blame food growers, processors, and food sellers when they get sick from eating contaminated food, she says. This shift, already seen in million-dollar settlements such as those against Holiday Inn at San Francisco's Fisherman's Wharf and Foodmaker, the parent company of Jack-in-the-Box, is making restaurant owners and grocers take extra steps to make sure the food they deliver or sell is as safe as it can be.

Even though consumers seem willing to buy irradiated food, "it will probably take some truly traumatic E. coli outbreak that causes a number of deaths before government and the food industry get serious about food irradiation," says James Tillotson of Tufts. Without such a crisis, consumers probably wouldn't think of demanding irradiated food and there would be little political push to require leaving companies that explore irradiation open to attack by activist groups such as Food and Water. "No one is willing to get that kind of attention," he says, "even when they might be doing the best thing for consumers."

8

Food Irradiation Is Dangerous and Ineffective

Susan Meeker-Lowry

Susan Meeker-Lowry is the author of Economics As If the Earth Really Mattered *and* Invested in the Common Good.

Irradiation is a misguided approach to food safety because it creates health problems, including cancer and kidney damage, and does not guarantee uncontaminated food. The workers at irradiation plants are especially at risk because of potential exposure to high doses of radiation. Irradiation is also dangerous because it can kill the foul-smelling molds and yeasts that indicate spoiled food, while leaving harmful bacteria in that food untouched. The solution to food-borne illnesses is to improve the conditions at packing plants and slaughterhouses, rather than to rely on irradiation.

If the U.S. Department of Agriculture (USDA), the nuclear industry, and the food industry have their way, nuking food to kill bacteria like e. coli and salmonella, and to extend its shelf-life will become standard operating procedure. While it is legal to zap fruits, vegetables, spices, grains, pork, and poultry with radiation, you haven't seen much of this irradiated food on the supermarket shelves (with the exception of spices) thanks in large part to campaigns opposing the process launched by organizations like Food & Water and thousands of consumers who don't like the idea of eating irradiated food. Thanks in large part to these campaigns, investors in food irradiation have lost their shirts: Food Technology Service, Inc. (FTSI) based in Mulberry, Florida (formerly known as Vindicator), the nation's first food irradiation facility, has posted over $5 million in losses since opening in 1992 because people don't like the idea of eating nuked chicken and vegetables. As a result, other companies were reluctant to jump on a bandwagon that promised only bankruptcy. But all that may change.

The FDA's imminent approval of beef irradiation has industry promoters salivating. [It was approved in December 1997.] Ever since several children died and hundreds were taken ill after eating e. coli contami-

Reprinted from Susan Meeker-Lowry, "From Irradiation to Electronic Pasteurization," *Z Magazine*, May 1996, with permission from the publisher.

nated hamburgers at a Jack-in-the-Box restaurant in 1993 (and in several other less publicized incidents), the USDA has been pushing for FDA approval of beef irradiation as one "solution" to the growing problem of meat contamination. While most people might balk at irradiating fruits and vegetables (very few people die from eating contaminated fruit, although harms caused by pesticide residues are all too real), the fact is our meat supply in this country is contaminated by dangerous pathogens.

E. coli is responsible for 500 deaths and 20,000 illnesses annually, and these numbers appear to be rising. Hamburger, which is easily contaminated is connected to 70 percent of e. coli outbreaks. Salmonella is responsible for almost 2 million poisonings each year in the U.S., resulting in up to 2,000 deaths. While you hear most about salmonella contaminating poultry, raw eggs, and raw milk, red meat is linked to a third of all salmonella outbreaks.

Taking advantage of the very real hazards in the nation's meat supply, irradiation promoters, working with the USDA, and researchers at major land grant universities in pro-irradiation departments, are busy at work creating "educational" materials (some call it "consumer training") for both meat industry execs and consumers. The meat industry has been reluctant to irradiate its products since people obviously don't want to eat irradiated meat. Plus it appears zapped meat simply doesn't taste that great. In 1994, *The Economist,* reporting on taste test research, said irradiated meat has a "burnt-hair taste—especially beef." To counter this negative publicity, thousands of dollars, much of it tax dollars, are being spent on promotional videos and related materials to influence the public to accept food irradiation.

Numerous animal studies indicate health problems associated with eating irradiated foods.

For example, scientists at Iowa State University (ISU), home to one of two publicly held food irradiation facilities in the U.S., are working on a video that they say will convince "at least 50 percent [of consumers who view it] . . . to purchase irradiated meat products." The video likens food irradiation to milk pasteurization, and features interviews with 15 scientists and government officials advocating the process. Opponents to irradiation were represented by two employees of Iowa food cooperatives and their remarks were limited to a few sentences. The USDA is taking the results of university consumer acceptance studies and projects like the one at ISU to meat industry executives to convince them it is possible to "win consumers' approval" of the irradiation process. Thanks to a pro-active campaign by Food & Water, International Beef Processors (IBP), the largest meat processing corporation in the U.S., came out against irradiation in March of 1996 when CEO Robert L. Peterson stated, "We at IBP do not irradiate any of our meat products, nor do we have plans to begin. We agree that current irradiation procedures can affect traditional meat flavors."

Still the USDA and the irradiation industry persist, joining forces with the state of Hawaii to promote the irradiation of Hawaiian fruit destined for U.S. and Japanese markets. So far, the main outlet for zapped Hawaiian fruit has been Carrot Top Market based in Chicago. Other purveyors of irradiated food include Sterigenics, a California-based irradiation company that markets its own brands of irradiated spices under the Purely by Choice label; and New Horizon Technology, Inc. (NHTI), a new commercial irradiation facility in Washington state founded by two scientists at the Department of Energy's (DoE) laboratories at Hanford (one of the largest nuclear waste dumps in the world) and FTSI. While founders raise the $5 million necessary to build their facility, NHTI has an agreement to use the DoE's cobalt-60 irradiator at Hanford. To get the venture off the ground New Horizon zapped 100 cases of Walla Walla sweet onions which are proudly featured in sandwiches sold in the Baron's Beef & Brew restaurant in Richland, WA. To "educate" skeptical customers, Baron's co-owner, Vicki Silvernail, compares an irradiated onion to a sunburned person.

Food irradiation has been around a long time—in 1916 Sweden first experimented with irradiation of strawberries and the first U.S. patents were taken out in 1921. In the 1950s, food irradiation was considered one of the atoms for peace technologies and in 1957 irradiation was first used on spices for sausage in Germany but was promptly banned the following year. In 1958, irradiation was classified as a food additive requiring safety testing but in 1976 this requirement was relaxed somewhat. The first irradiation permits were issued in 1963 for wheat, potatoes, and bacon, and in 1990 for raw poultry.

Today, food irradiation is approved in 37 countries on over 40 products although it is actually used in only 18 countries and very sparingly at that. It has been endorsed by the United Nation's Food and Agriculture Organization (FAO) and the World Health Organization (WHO) as an important solution to the problem of food losses due to insect pests, food spoilage, and microbial contamination. (WHO's approval provoked considerable controversy which continues to this day. WHO did not undertake any studies, nor did they consult members.) In the U.S., potatoes, poultry, wheat, spices, dried vegetables, and pork can all be irradiated. While the FDA requires that irradiated foods be labeled, if only some ingredients are irradiated (spices in a sauce, for example) the label requirement is waived.

In the U.S. the FDA recommends general irradiation be permitted only up to the lower dose of 100,000 rad with the exception of spices which are permitted up to 3 million rad. In practice, however, there is the possibility foods will be zapped with much higher doses. Vice President of McCormick & Company (the spice company) R.L. Hall stated, "In existing large-scale irradiators, it is quite likely that an overdose of up to 250 percent can be expected."

Problems with irradiation

Irradiation disrupts the organic processes that lead to food decay. Proponents like it because it destroys bacteria, kills some insect pests, and extends the shelf life of foods. They gloss over the problems, implying that the threats posed by microbial contamination are greater than those posed by irradiation. Food is irradiated either by being exposed to large doses of ionizing radiation from radioactive gamma sources (cobalt-60 is used today, although cesium-137 was also used until 1988), or to extremely high energy electron beams (e-beams). Irradiated food is not rendered radioactive.

Gamma rays have sufficient energy to knock electrons out of the atoms, breaking the molecular structure of the food which results in positively and negatively charged particles called free radicals. Free radicals react with the food to create new chemical substances called "unique radiolytic products" (URPs). While some URPs may not be harmful, others, such as formaldehyde, benzene, formic acid, glyoxal, malondialdehyde, lipid peroxides, and quinones are definitely cause for concern. Benzene, for example, is known to cause cancer. In one experiment benzene was found to be over seven times higher in cooked, irradiated beef than in cooked, non-irradiated beef. Unfortunately, benzene is excluded from consideration by the FDA as a hazard accompanying irradiation because it is also generated by charcoal broiling. Some URPs are completely new chemicals that have not been identified, let alone tested for toxicity. Irradiation also destroys vitamins including vitamin A, some Bs, C, and E. Amino acids and fats may also be altered by the process.

Numerous animal studies indicate health problems associated with eating irradiated foods. *Public Citizen* details several in a document sent to the USDA's Food Safety Inspection Service (FSIS) regarding irradiation of poultry products in 1992. One in particular, carried out by Raltech Scientific Services, Inc. under contract with the U.S. government (actually twelve studies in one) examined the effect of feeding irradiated chicken to several different animal species. Results indicated the possibility of chromosome damage, immunetoxicity, greater incidence of kidney disease, cardiac thrombus, and fibroplasia. In reviewing Raltech's findings, Donald Thayer, a USDA researcher stated in 1984 that ". . . a collective assessment of study results argues against a definative [sic] conclusion that the gamma-irradiated test material [irradiated chicken meat] was free of toxic properties." Other studies on rats fed irradiated food also indicate possible kidney damage as well as testicular damage and a statistically significant increase in testicular tumors.

Contrary to what we are told, irradiation will not ensure uncontaminated food.

While irradiation proponents claim decades of research demonstrate the safety of the process, many (if not most) of the studies used to prove their point are questionable. Some were undertaken by the U.S. Army to obtain approval from the FDA for can-packed bacon in 1963, approval withdrawn in 1968 after the FDA discovered the research to be flawed. Others include those completed by Industrial Bio-Test (IBT), a firm convicted in 1983 of performing fraudulent research for government and industry. The army (one of their clients) discovered "missing records, unallowable departures from testing protocol, poor quality work, and incomplete disclosure of information on the progress of the studies." As a result of IBT's violations, the government lost about $4 million and 6 years worth of animal feeding study data on food irradiation. Some of this discredited work is still used as part of the "scientific" basis for assurances of the safety of food irradiation today.

The FDA's assessment before the approval of pork irradiation, was also seriously flawed. The agency included 5 of 441 available toxicity studies, since only those 5 were "properly conducted, fully adequate by 1980 toxicological standards, and able to stand alone in support of safety." Why the FDA relied on even the remaining five is baffling since when they were reviewed by the Department of Preventative Medicine and Community Health of the New Jersey Medical School, two were found to be methodologically flawed. Two others appeared to be sound, but investigated the effects of diets consisting of foods treated to lower doses than what the FDA currently approves. Further, two of the studies they chose to include did indicate problems with irradiation—one suggesting that irradiated food could have adverse effects on older animals, and the other showing that animals fed a diet of irradiated foods experienced weight loss and miscarriage, most likely due to irradiation-induced vitamin E deficiency. Yet the agency ignored these possible negative impacts on health. Further damning the FDA's work, Marcia van Gemert, the toxicologist and chair of the FDA committee that investigated the 441 studies and wrote the final report in 1982 recently wrote in a letter dated October 19, 1993, "These studies . . . were not adequate by 1982 standards, and are even less adequate by 1993 standards to evaluate the safety of any product, especially a food product such as irradiated foods."

Workers in irradiation plants could be exposed to extremely large doses of radiation.

Contrary to what we are told, irradiation will not ensure uncontaminated food. While it kills most bacteria, it does not remove the toxins created in the early stages of contamination. In any case, not all microorganisms in food are bad. Some smell awful, letting us know food is spoiled, others, such as yeasts and molds, compete with harmful bacteria and provide a natural control on their growth. Since some bacteria may not be destroyed by irradiation, it will be easier for the survivors to multiply unchecked, and there will be no putrid smell to indicate spoilage. For example, current doses of radiation are not powerful enough to kill c. botulinum in chicken. It does, however, kill most of the yeasts and molds that naturally compete with it along with most of the organisms that indicate spoilage by smelling bad. Under the right conditions c. botulinum will multiply and become a health hazard with no warning odor to indicate toxicity. It's a fact that irradiation has a mutagenic effect on the bacteria and viruses that survive zapping. These mutated survivors may be resistant to antibiotics or could evolve into more virulent strains of microorganisms. They could also become radiation-resistant and if released into the environment, could contaminate food prior to irradiation rendering the process ineffective. Radiation resistant mutants of salmonella have been developed by repeated irradiation under laboratory conditions, and resistant strains have also been found in environments with high natural or artificial radiation.

Scientists at Louisiana State University recently found one bacteria occurring in spoiled meat and animal feces that can survive a dose of radiation five times what the FDA approved for beef. The bacteria, D. radiodurans, was exposed to between 10 and 15 kilograys (kGy) of radiation for several hours—enough to kill a person several thousand times over. Scientists speculate the bacteria's resistance to radiation could have originated from desiccation or prolonged dehydration, which has the same destructive impact on chromosomes as radiation. Jennifer Ferrara, with Food & Water, says, "This discovery raises serious doubts about the propriety of a technology that may accelerate the evolution of already harmful bacteria into still deadlier strains. Will a radiation-resistant, super-salmonella be next?"

Proponents of irradiation do not dispute that the process damages many vitamins, specifically A, many of the Bs (thiamine, B2, B3, B6, B12, folic acid), C, E, and K. Essential polyunsaturated fatty acids are also affected. The extent of loss depends on the type of food and the radiation dose. Generally the more complex the food, the less it suffers. Still a 20 percent to 80 percent loss is not uncommon. The justifications for irradiation in light of such significant vitamin loss are: irradiated foods probably won't be a huge percentage of anyone's diet; or in countries experiencing extreme hunger, at least it's food.

Radiation can be dangerous

Workers in irradiation plants could be exposed to extremely large doses of radiation due to equipment failure, leaking, or accidental exposure to the source—just like workers in nuclear power plants. The irradiation chamber requires constant maintenance and upkeep since it is a very corrosive atmosphere, increasing the likelihood of exposure, and irradiation sources will have to be produced, transported, stored, and installed, then replaced when depleted.

While advocates of irradiation maintain the safety of the technology, the Nuclear Regulatory Commission (NRC) has recorded 54 accidents at 132 irradiation facilities since 1974. This number is probably low because about 30 states have agreements with the NRC to monitor and enforce regulations of irradiation facilities themselves. The NRC has no information on incidents in these states. (This agreement does not apply to nuclear power plants, which are monitored by the NRC). Here are a few of the reported accidents:

• In 1974, whistleblowers at the Isomedix company in New Jersey reported that radioactive water was flushed down toilets and had contaminated pipes leading to sewers. The same year a worker received a dose of radiation considered lethal—prompt hospital treatment saved his life.

• In 1982, International Nutronics in Dover, New Jersey, a company that used radiation baths to purify gems, chemicals, food, and medical supplies had an accident that completely contaminated the plant forcing its closure. A pump malfunctioned siphoning water from the baths onto the floor. The contaminated water was dumped down the drain into the Dover sewer system. The NRC wasn't informed of the accident until ten months later—and then by a whistleblower, not the company. In 1986, the company and one of its top executives were convicted by a federal jury of conspiracy and fraud. Radiation has been detected in the vicinity of the plant, but the NRC claims the levels "aren't hazardous." The plant was located in a heavily populated area.

• In 1986, the NRC revoked the license of a Radiation Technology, Inc. (RTI) plant (also in New Jersey) for repeated worker safety violations. (RTI was the company that petitioned the FDA for permission to irradiate pork, granted in 1985). RTI was cited 32 times for various violations, including throwing radioactive garbage out with the regular trash. The most serious violation was bypassing a safety device to prevent people from entering the irradiation chamber during operation resulting in a worker receiving a near lethal dose of radiation.

• In 1988, Radiation Sterilizers (RSI) in Decatur, Georgia, reported a leak of cesium-137 which had been provided by the DoE from their weapons' production facility in Hanford, Washington, to sterilize medical supplies and treat food. In addition to contaminating the plant and endangering workers, medical supplies and consumer products were contaminated. The supposedly "fail-proof" cesium-137 capsules leaked into the water storage pool. Officials found "extensive" radiation contamination throughout the facility. In addition, inspections of plant workers' homes and cars found that radioactivity had been transported outside the facility. RSI had intended to use cobalt-60, but changed to cesium-137 because the cobalt was unavailable. In 1985, when RSI requested the cesium, the NRC expressed serious reservations regarding the durability of the cesium capsules, fearing corrosion and leakage could occur if they were repeatedly immersed into water. As a result, RSI was given permission to use the capsules as a trial for one year only. After just one month of use, the DoE claimed the capsules were safe and the NRC reversed its decision. Clean-up costs exceeded $30 million. After this incident, irradiation facilities stopped using cesium-137 in favor of cobalt-60.

Unfortunately, all the debate about zapping food with e-beams or radioactive isotopes, does nothing to solve the very real food safety crisis in this country.

Sometimes containers of radioactive material are found where they have no business being. For example a young boy found a cobalt-60 source in a Mexican dump, brought it home where it sat on a shelf irradiating the family, eventually leading to the deaths of everyone living in the home, including his grandmother, his mother, and his sister. Radioactive sources have been known to leak out of the facilities where they are being used, as well. Four gallon jugs containing radioactive tritium leaked onto a sidewalk outside of the Johns Hopkins Hospital in Maryland in 1981. In Arizona, the American Atomics plant was responsible for leaking 284,000 curies of tritium gas into the atmosphere in 1978 alone. This contaminated food served to 40,000 school children, the city sewer system, and swimming pools in the area.

In 1993 the NRC fined the Department of Agriculture for repeatedly violating numerous radiation safety guidelines at more than 20 research sites. According to *The New York Times*, the repeat violations included the USDA's failure to inspect laboratories, test for leakage, and keep material securely stored. Other violations included failing to train certain workers, letting unauthorized people handle radioactive material, and using an irradiator on blood, grasshoppers, and spiders without first obtaining authorization.

There have been numerous documented incidents of radioactive sources being lost or damaged during transit. Some are safely recovered, others are discovered by unsuspecting passersby, and others simply disappear. Since the general belief at this time is that food will be irradiated using cobalt-60, despite its limited availability, because it is considered safer than cesium-137, my inquiry in this area was limited to incidents involving shipments of cobalt-60 in recent years (since 1988). The Transportation Development Department of Sandia National Laboratories, which keeps track of all reported incidents involving radioactive materials, sent about a dozen "incident reports" involving cobalt-60. As Cheryl Crockett at Sandia explained, "It is possible there may be more [accidents] than what I collect due to unclear information about what was transported." In other words, not all accidents involving radioactive materials are reported to the authorities.

While it is not possible to compute significant statistics from such a limited number of reports, it appears safe to say that most accidents involving radioactive materials result in some kind of damage or contamination (75 percent of the accidents in this case). What is more surprising is how often the radioactive source is lost and never recovered. For example, in 1993 a Cessna carrying cobalt-60 in a steel drum with a lead shield crashed into Mt. Taylor in New Mexico. All four occupants of the plane were killed and the cobalt-60 has not been recovered. It is believed to be buried under eight feet of snow. In 1991 two containers of cobalt-60 were not delivered to Berthold Systems in Pennsylvania. How do officials decide that "the potential exposure hazard to the public is expected to be minimal" when no one knows where they are? In another instance a ten foot long rod of cobalt-60 was missing from a package received by Berthold Systems. It was later discovered under a dumpster outside a cargo building at JFK Airport. The report states, "Evidently, the padlock which secures the cylinder latch was lost. It is not known where, when, or how the padlock was lost."

Irradiation and nuclear byproducts

While irradiation proponents like to distance themselves from the Department of Energy (DoE) and issues related to nuclear weapons, energy, and waste, the DoE was one of the first developers and promoters of food irradiation through its Byproducts Utilization Program (BUP). BUP was created in the 1970s to promote the use of nuclear byproducts which the DoE claimed "have a wide range of applications in food technology, agriculture, energy, public health, medicine, and industrial technology. . . . Transfer of this federally-developed technology to industry will ensure full realization of the benefits of the peaceful atom."

DoE's reason for promoting nuclear byproducts was made clear at hearings held in 1983 before the House Armed Services Committee: ". . . the utilization of these radioactive materials simply reduces our waste handling problem . . . we get some of these very hot elements like cesium and strontium out of the waste." The DoE was particularly keen on developing technology to reprocess spent nuclear reactor fuel in order to recover the cesium-137 (and plutonium, although this wasn't loudly discussed) and it actively promoted the development of food irradiation using cesium-137 for years. According to the DoE in 1983, "The strategy being pursued . . . is designed to transfer federally developed cesium-137 irradiation technology to the commercial sector as rapidly and successfully as possible. The measure of success will be the degree to which this technology is implemented industrially and the subsequent demand created for cesium-137." Today there are about 50 irradiation plants in the U.S., mostly for medical purposes, and about 130 irradiation facilities world wide. Since the accident involving cesium-137 capsules in Decatur, Georgia, in 1988, cobalt-60 has been used exclusively in irradiation facilities. Cobalt-60 is manufactured by placing nonradioactive cobalt-59 in the core of a nuclear reactor for about 18 months. A Canadian company, Nordion International, Inc. supplies about 90 percent of the world's industrial cobalt and can't keep up with the demand.

The only isotope available in sufficient quantities for the kind of large-scale irradiation that would be necessary to zap all hamburger is cesium-137, one of the most abundantly available radioactive wastes—and also one of the deadliest. With a half-life of 30 years, cesium-137 remains dangerous for about 600 years. In order to obtain cesium-137 from spent commercial reactor fuel, it must first be reprocessed. (Plutonium is another "by-product" of reprocessing spent reactor fuel.)

Neither the government nor industry currently claim to have plans for the use of cesium-137 in irradiation facilities—although *Food Chemical News* (1/8/96) reported that some companies objected to a petition brought before the FDA to approve the use of cobalt-60 to treat poultry feed because it didn't also approve the use of cesium-137. The companies were urged to withdraw their objections and file a food additive petition for the use of cesium-137.

Unsafe electron beams

Due to the shortage of cobalt-60 and the dangers inherent in using cesium-137, irradiation proponents are latching on to linear accelerators which are thought to be safer because they require no radioactive isotopes. Linear accelerators use a high power electron beam to x-ray food. Dennis Olsen, an expert on this technology, says their advantage is they have such high power levels the food needs to be exposed for a very short time (zapping with cobalt-60 takes hours, he said). One of the major disadvantages of electron beam irradiation is the potential of induced radioactivity. According to the Council for Agricultural Science and Technology's 1986 report on food irradiation, "Radioactivity can be induced if the energy level is great enough." According to Olsen, "You need 14 to 15 million electron volts (MEVs) before food becomes radioactive. Most e-beam machines can't go beyond 10 million electron volts." Even so Olsen didn't think linear accelerators were very practical for food because their "penetration is small—only about one and a half inches on each side." There are also concerns regarding refrigeration since MEVs need to be at room temperature and for safety reasons food needs to be chilled.

Electron beam enthusiasts claim the technology is much safer for workers than conventional irradiation. According to Roy Hamil of Sandia Labs, "If there is a problem you just push the 'off' switch." But, as a worker at a Maryland e-beam facility discovered on December 11, 1991, it's not that simple. An employee turned the machine off to begin a maintenance check. However, e-beam machines are subject to a phenomenon known as "cold" or "dark" current, meaning that an electron beam can be present even when the voltage is turned off. The operator spent between one and three minutes with his head, hands, and feet directly in the beam's path. The day after the accident the victim's fingers began to turn red, swell, and become very painful. Two weeks later, he had lost all function in both hands, had sores and blistering on his feet, face, and scalp, and had to be hospitalized for severe pain. Three months later it was necessary to amputate four fingers on his right hand and most of four fingers on his left hand.

In addition, there have been numerous reports of accidents at medical centers using e-beams to treat cancer patients. In 1991, a malfunctioning e-beam constructed by General Electric-CGR killed five cancer patients at a medical facility in Spain. In the U.S., in 1986, two cancer patients were killed by a malfunctioning electron beam irradiator in Texas.

But industry is pushing it. To make it more acceptable to the public the process is called "electronic pasteurization." Sounds very 21st century. A recent article in *The Packer* touts e-beams for the quarantine treatment of fruits and vegetables coming in from Mexico. According to the DoE's Sandia Labs, such a facility could produce 900 tons of produce a day on standard pallets. The article declares that "a market might exist for as many as 30 plants for produce and other foods." It goes on to state that, "These kinds of facilities also could be built to increase produce shelf life, sterilize products, and kill or control bacteria in meats, hamburger, poultry, shellfish, and other perishables."

In terms of food safety, e-beams do the exact same damage to food as radioactive sources. Dr. Walter Burnstein, founder and president of Food & Water states, "People don't like to be tricked, and that's clearly what irradiation proponents are trying to do with electron beams. It's clearly a case of putting old wine in new bottles, and it still doesn't taste good." Ironically, Japanese scientists, in a desperate attempt to find some use for food irradiation technology, want to use doses of radiation strong enough to kill 250 people to make bad wine taste better and cheap whiskey smoother. "It's funny," said Hiroshi Watanabe, joint head of research at the Japan Atomic Power Co.'s research facilities in Takasaki, "if you irradiate good wine or whiskey, they taste terrible. But if you expose bad wine and cheap whiskey to gamma rays, they taste better." Unfortunately, all the debate about zapping food with e-beams or radioactive isotopes, does nothing to solve the very real food safety crisis in this country. The problem goes right back to the highly concentrated nature of the meat industry and the abhorrent conditions in the feed lots, slaughter houses, and packing plants. What's needed is a local/regional approach to food systems. If you want to be part of the solution oppose industry's magic bullets (like irradiation), let your supermarket know how you feel about irradiation and pesticides, and support your local farmer and food co-op.

9

Biotechnology Can Improve Food Safety and Quality

Susanne L. Huttner

*Susanne L. Huttner is the director of the University of California Sys-
temwide Biotechnology Research and Education Program.*

Biotechnology, the use of living organisms to make or modify
products, benefits food safety and quality in a variety of ways. For
example, scientists have developed antibodies that target food
contaminants. Biotechnology techniques improve the quality of
crops and livestock by reducing the damaging effects of viruses
and bacteria and by enhancing taste and nutrition. Because these
techniques have been proven safe, biotechnology foods do not require labeling or premarket testing.

New biotechnology techniques hold real promise for American agriculture and for consumers in at least six important ways, some of
which are discussed in more detail below:
1. Biotechnology can improve the quality—e.g., the flavor, nutritional value or productive efficiency—of American crops and livestock.
2. Biotechnology can allow early detection and treatment of disease
or infestation of food crops and animals.
3. Biotechnology can reduce the need for chemical pesticides through
the introduction of internal biological mechanisms to combat pest
and disease damage of crops.
4. Biotechnology can improve food processing and fermentation
systems.
5. Biotechnology can improve detection of food contaminants that
could pose a threat to health.
6. Biotechnology can open new markets for American agricultural
products.
The new techniques extend the reach of plant breeders. Crop scientists can now seek beneficial traits—pest and disease resistance, drought
and salt tolerance and factors that enhance the nutritional quality of

Excerpted from Susanne L. Huttner's paper, "Biotechnology and Food," prepared for the American
Council on Science and Health, January 1996, available at http://www.acsh.org/publications/
booklets/biotechnology.html. Reprinted with permission from the publisher.

fruits and vegetables—theoretically, wherever they exist in nature. The new traits are brought into more rapid service to improve agriculture and food production.

American agriculture is seriously challenged by the growing governmental restriction of pesticides; by continuing environmental stresses, including drought and soil salinity; and by the need to conserve and restore lands. Biotechnology cannot, by itself, address all of these challenges, but researchers are developing many new varieties of food crops that provide improvements that will help relieve some of the problems.

Improved quality

From disease-resistant crops to produce that stays fresh longer, agricultural biotechnology holds promise for improving the food we eat in ways that benefit both farmers and consumers. New varieties of crop plants fall into four basic categories of improvements: 1) enhanced food quality, 2) disease- or pest-resistance, 3) environmental stress tolerance and 4) weed management.

More than 90 bioengineered plants derived from 20 different crops are currently being developed. Biotechnology also affords interesting new approaches to protecting animal health—approaches that will affect both American farmers and consumers. The following is a brief look at some of the more significant new applications of biotechnology in American agriculture.

Selective genetic alterations can significantly enhance the appearance, flavor, texture and nutrition of foods from plants and animals. Genes for nutritionally important seed proteins are being introduced into plants that lack essential amino acids. Rice, corn and other staple grains are being made more nutritionally balanced and healthful.

The introduction of genes for enzymes involved in starch metabolism increases the starch levels in potatoes in order to reduce fat absorption during frying. Genes for enzymes that determine the sugar and solid content of tomatoes improve their flavor and processing quality. A variety of canola (rapeseed) oil has been modified to improve its fat profile.

Genes involved in the natural metabolic pathways that lead to fruit softening and rotting are being genetically altered to ensure that fruits and vegetables reach our supermarket shelves as near to the peak of ripeness and flavor as possible. The FlavrSavr® tomato is the first example of genetically engineered produce introduced to the fresh market.

Pest and weed control

The economic, health and environmental costs associated with not controlling pests are staggering. In response, we are seeing a growing movement to support the development of biological strategies for controlling pests. New strategies for pest and disease control are particularly important for food production with small acreage, for "minor-use" crops and in developing countries. There is an immediate, worldwide need for carefully tailored pest-control strategies of the sort biotechnology can create.

Crops can be made naturally resistant to the damaging effects of insects or pathogens (like viruses) by introducing single genes that confer protection against the pests. Many farmers have relied upon selected classes of microorganisms to fight certain insects. These microorganisms kill selectively and are safe for humans, animals and other beneficial insects. They have the unfortunate characteristic, however, of being easily washed away and so must be frequently reapplied. Researchers have been exploring ways in which the insect-fighting gene might be integrated directly into the plant, thereby conferring natural protection and reducing the need for repeated applications of microorganisms or chemical pesticides.

The bacterium *Bacillus thuringiensis* (Bt) is a common biological control agent that has been used by American farmers for decades. Bt produces a protein that selectively kills certain classes of crop-damaging insects. The gene for the protein has been identified and transferred to plants. For example, walnut trees have been protected against navel orange worm, Indian meal moth and other insects by the simple addition of the Bt gene. The Bt gene has also been transferred to cotton, corn, rapeseed (canola), rice, tomato and potato. Cotton alone accounts for about 40 percent of all chemical pesticide use in the United States. Adding the Bt gene to the cotton plant can reduce chemical pesticide needs by 10 percent or more.

Viral diseases are another important problem addressed by biotechnology. Viral infections drastically reduce crop yields throughout America and have been essentially untreatable. They are controlled primarily by applying insecticides that kill the insects that carry the viruses to the plants.

Agricultural biotechnology holds promise for improving the food we eat.

New molecular approaches enable plant breeders to identify antiviral strategies that exist in nature. Researchers have found, for example, that by transferring a single gene from a virus into a plant, they can effectively protect the plant against future infection by that virus. This strategy is proving effective against a wide variety of viruses that affect potatoes, cucumbers, squash, melons and legumes. The first virus-resistant squash are expected in the marketplace shortly. Aphids and leafhoppers that carry the virus from plant to plant are usually controlled by chemical pesticides; the new virus-resistant squash will eliminate the need for those chemical treatments.

Fungal diseases present yet another troublesome problem. They cause enormous crop losses in the United States. Moreover, certain fungi produce aflatoxin, a proven human carcinogen. Biological strategies for controlling fungal contamination are under development using modern genetic techniques.

Early treatment of plant disease is an important strategy for reducing chemical inputs in American farming. The new biotechnology offers highly sensitive and selective diagnostic tools to detect low levels of infection or infestation. This is essential for speeding the delivery of control measures before the problem grows. Field kits based on antibodies that specifically recognize a disease or pest agent are already in use for soybean root rot and certain bacterial diseases of tomatoes and grapes. Deoxyribonucleic acid (DNA) fingerprinting—famous for its use in forensics—is also used in identifying plant diseases and infestations.

Herbicides are a common and widespread tool for reducing damage from weeds that invade crop fields. The challenge is to develop sustainable weed control agents that meet farmers' converging needs for cost-effective strategies that are also environmentally sound and free from health concerns. One approach involves using new herbicides that can be applied in lower doses with the same or improved weed control effects. Researchers and breeders are developing genetically modified crops that enable farmers to use these new, safer herbicides in smaller amounts. These crops enable farmers to reduce chemical inputs to their fields, reduce pesticide runoff and protect water supplies.

Drought, flooding, soil salinity, frost and other environmental stresses take heavy tolls on agricultural production in the United States. Several of the genes involved in plant responses to these stressors have been identified, and researchers are studying ways in which they can be used to enable food crops to withstand environmental challenges. Strategies under study include genetic alterations that would increase the rigidity of plant stalks and reduce drought-induced damage from wilting and droop.

The use of biotechnology on animals

Biotechnology's dramatic accomplishments in human health can often be extended directly to animal health and to the use of animals in food production. Just as new biotechnology diagnostics and therapeutics can help us detect and treat human diseases, they can provide a strategy for controlling animal diseases. Just as biotechnology research tools can help us identify useful genes and metabolic processes, they can help us improve the production and quality of foods derived from animals. A few examples follow.

By identifying and mapping genes, veterinary scientists are able to understand and help correct the physiological systems that underlie animal diseases. The identification of genes involved in serious inherited diseases helps animal breeders select the healthiest animals and improve the characteristics of their herds. Genetic diagnostic kits are becoming commonplace in animal husbandry.

New biotechnology vaccines are also playing important roles in veterinary medicine—both in the United States and in developing countries where more stable animal food production systems are of critical importance. One genetically engineered vaccine successfully controls Rinderpest, a viral disease that periodically destroys entire cattle herds in Africa and Asia. Another biotechnology vaccine has proved effective against rabies virus in trials in the eastern United States.

The genetic engineering of food animals is in the earliest stages of development. Most research, with a few notable exceptions (such as bovine somatotropin), is very preliminary and will require extensive development before genetically engineered meats reach the marketplace.

Genetic engineering can be used to improve the metabolic efficiency of animals, thereby enhancing the utilization of feed and improving meat and milk production. Bovine somatotropin (bST, also called bovine growth hormone, or bGH) is a natural protein hormone that stimulates and improves the efficiency of milk production in cows. The cow's gene for bST has been identified and used to produce the hormone. The genetically engineered bST is identical to the cow's own bST. When injected into dairy cows, the genetically engineered hormone increases milk production by the same mechanism as the cow's own bST. Dairy farmers have found that injecting bST also increases the efficiency of feed utilization, resulting in more milk and less manure produced per unit of feed consumed. The use of bST in milk production has been carefully evaluated and approved by the U.S. Food and Drug Administration (FDA) and by other regulatory agencies in more than 30 countries.

Biotechnology's dramatic accomplishments in human health can often be extended directly to animal health.

[Note: Early concerns of opponents of biotechnology about the healthfulness of milk from bST-treated cows led to extensive research. After more than eight years of analysis, it has been found that milk from bST-treated cows is indistinguishable from milk from untreated cows, both in composition and wholesomeness. Whether high production was achieved by bST injection, by improving the feed or by selective breeding, high-production cows occasionally develop mastitis, an infection of the udder related to frequent milking. It can be controlled with common antibiotics. Concerns about antibiotic residues in milk from high-production cows are addressed by the FDA. The agency requires that animals treated with antibiotics be kept out of milk production during the treatment period and for a certain amount of time after treatment has ended.]

Animal hormones can also affect the percentage of fat contained in meat. Administration of growth hormone to growing cattle or pigs substantially reduces the amount of fat and increases the proportion of lean, edible tissue.

Biotechnology and processed foods

Processed foods have gained acceptance among time-conscious American consumers in search of easy-to-prepare, nutritious and flavorful meals. Three components of the food-processing system are targeted by new biotechnologies: 1) chemical composition (such as proteins, fats and carbohydrates; see previous section); 2) bacteria and yeast used in fermentation and other processes; and 3) enzymes used to enhance color, flavor and texture.

Starter cultures of bacteria and yeast are the mainstay of much of the processed-food industry. Biotechnology has contributed substantially to microbial genetics, improving our understanding of bacterial and yeast genes that are involved in making foods as diverse as bread, yogurt, cheese, wine and beer. Using modern genetics, food processors are culturing new strains of microorganisms that have combinations of enzymes useful in food processing.

Biotechnology is also useful in the isolation and production of enzymes used directly in food processing. For example, the enzyme amylase affects the texture and freshness of bread dough. Chymosin, the active enzyme in rennin extracts (which are isolated from calf stomach), curdles milk to make cheese. Purified chymosin produced through genetic engineering now accounts for the majority of enzyme used in cheese production in the United States. Other enzymes, like proteases and lipases, are used to provide the aged quality of cheese.

There is also an effort to help meet consumer demands for foods that can be kept fresh without synthetic additives or special packaging materials. Biotechnology research is addressing the natural metabolic processes that affect freshness—for example, controlling ripening enzymes in the FlavrSavr® tomato to reduce early softening and allow fruit to ripen on the vine. Modern molecular methods are being used to produce substances that eliminate bacterial contamination, including propionic acid to reduce fungal contamination, trehalose sugars for dried and frozen foods and antioxidant enzymes to prevent free-radical formation. Other researchers are developing methods for enhancing the vitamin C and E content of processed foods.

Strategies derived from our knowledge of the mammalian immune system are being applied to food-production problems. The immune system attacks foreign molecules in the body by producing highly selective antibodies that identify and help destroy invaders. Exploiting that defense system, food scientists have developed antibodies that specifically target food contaminants that are potentially toxic or pathogenic. These new detection systems are being tested and packaged in easy-to-use kits. Food producers and handlers will be able to identify and eliminate contaminated foods before they reach supermarket shelves.

Biotechnology and biodiversity

The world population is expected to reach 10 billion people in the first half of the 21st century. Much of the growth is occurring in developing countries, where local capacity for food production is made seriously unstable by poverty, political disruption, climatic stresses, soil erosion, pests and disease. The pace at which primitive forests and other natural lands are being converted to food production is increasing, but it can be slowed. When biotechnology is used in combination with other strategies, it can help us address several of the central problems. The new molecular tools are both enhancing our understanding of the range and importance of biodiversity and supporting strategies that will spare and even return land to natural habitats while helping to feed the world's peoples.

We have learned from the Green Revolution of the 1970s, with its introduction of high-yield wheat and rice varieties, that carefully targeted plant breeding can substantially improve local food production. The new genetic tools can both enhance and extend those improvements by delivering technological enhancements directly, in the seed. Biotechnology research is under way in agricultural centers in South and Central America, the Caribbean, Africa, Asia and the Pacific Islands. Much of this research focuses on crops that are important for rural farmers—rice, beans, maize, squash, melons, cassava, papaya, sorghum, potatoes and sweet potatoes. Superior varieties will help farmers achieve greater yields with lower inputs on less land.

Biotechnology offers novel products to replace those derived from forestry or agriculture. Biomaterials are under development to reduce our reliance on fiber- and petroleum-based products. Plant cells can be grown in large-scale vats, or bioreactors, to make products ranging from oils to flavorings and amino acids without cultivating land. These approaches all help to reduce the need to bring greater acreage under cultivation and reduce the need to harvest the world's forests.

The genetic engineering of food animals is in the earliest stages of development.

The world today supports a remarkable diversity of plant and animal life. This diversity is the source both of esthetic enjoyment and of the fruits, vegetables and animal-derived foods available in our supermarkets. For centuries, plant and animal breeders have sought the best traits from wild species and genetically integrated them into domesticated crops and food animals. Extensive seed banks—literally, gene banks—have been established to collect a broad range of germplasm both to document and characterize the world's various species and to support future breeding needs. Thus, an appreciation and utilization of biodiversity has been a hallmark of traditional plant and animal breeding programs around the world.

Biotechnology offers several strategies for sustaining and utilizing the world's biodiversity. First, it offers tools for identifying and characterizing living organisms at the genetic level. Molecular diagnostic techniques enable scientists to distinguish between and compare species with remarkable precision. Used in combination with traditional techniques, genetic engineering techniques are expanding our knowledge of the range and evolution of organisms living in American meadows and tropical rain forests alike. They allow researchers to monitor and track changes in specific populations over time. Knowledge of the genetic composition of wild species also enables breeders to identify and make use of genes that encode traits that are beneficial for food production.

The safety of genetically engineered foods

The potential markets for new biotechnology products are virtually as broad as those for more conventional agricultural and food products. In fact, it is hard to imagine a sector of the food production system that will not be affected by new biotechnologies over the next decade.

The prospects for achieving the full potential impact of the new technologies depend upon a number of factors, however. Those factors include private-sector investment, government regulations and consumer acceptance. The history of agricultural biotechnology is markedly different from that of biomedical applications of biotechnology, where tens of millions of Americans have already benefited directly from diagnostics and therapeutics. Medical products have been moving relatively rapidly from the bench to commercial application, while agricultural products have moved much more slowly. This is due, in part, to the fact that basic plant sciences have been much less well funded, historically, than has biomedical research. A great deal of fundamental genetics research had to be completed before the first plants could be successfully engineered.

Perhaps more important, however, has been the effect of continuing controversy over agricultural applications of biotechnology—starting with the struggle over the first field tests of the "ice minus," a bacterium modified to reduce frost damage in farmers' fields, in California in the 1980s and continuing with the current debate over the labeling of new biotechnology foods.

An important determinant of the future of food biotechnology may lie in the federal government's decision on food labeling. Although the FDA announced in 1991 that labels would not be required for all food products of biotechnology, certain activist organizations continue to call for mandatory labels such as "genetically engineered food" or "product of biotechnology."

The two most prominent controversies regarding biotechnology—the safety of the new techniques and product labeling—are fairly straightforward and have been addressed by numerous scientific and regulatory bodies in the United States and other countries. The concerns and findings are briefly summarized here.

Biotechnology offers several strategies for sustaining and utilizing the world's biodiversity.

Are genetic engineering techniques in any way inherently dangerous or unpredictable? The National Academy of Sciences, the National Research Council and numerous international scientific organizations have all emphasized that the new single-gene techniques are both precise and reliable (see Table 1). These organizations recommend that safety determinations focus on the nature of the trait that is introduced into a plant or animal. This is the approach that the FDA currently follows. New biotechnology foods are judged according to the same criteria as similar foods produced using more traditional methods.

The genetic engineering of crops and food has been more carefully scrutinized by the federal government than any crop-breeding technology in the history of American agriculture. Over the past 20 years, millions of laboratory experiments have been conducted with recombinant DNA (rDNA) techniques and with rDNA-modified organisms. There have been more than 1,000 field experiments with rDNA-modified plants throughout the world.

The genetic and phenotypic characteristics of every new genetically engineered plant are evaluated at each stage of development—laboratory, greenhouse and small-scale field trial—under guidelines and regulations of the National Institutes of Health (NIH), the U.S. Department of Agriculture (USDA), the Environmental Protection Agency (EPA) and the FDA. There is no evidence that rDNA techniques or rDNA-modified organisms pose any unique or unforeseen environmental or health hazards.

Common sense dictates that, compared to traditional breeding processes that affect hundreds of thousands of genes, transferring single genes greatly enhances our ability to judge risk and safety. Greater certainty about the genetic modification means greater accuracy in safety assessments.

Table 1: What Experts Say about Genetically Engineered Products

Findings of the National Academy of Sciences (1987):
"There is no evidence of the existence of unique hazards either in the use of rDNA techniques or in the movement of genes between unrelated organisms."

"The risks associated with the introduction of rDNA-engineered organisms are the same in kind as those associated with the introduction of unmodified organisms and organisms modified by other methods."

Findings of the National Research Council (1989):
"No conceptual distinction exists between genetic modification of plants and microorganisms by classical methods or by molecular techniques that modify DNA or transfer genes."

Findings of the National Research Council (1987):
"Because the genetic change is better characterized than those achieved with classical breeding, safety issues related to the changes made can be addressed more precisely."

Some people wonder whether the source of a gene affects the safety of foods. Given the tremendous overlap in genes among humans, animals, plants and even microorganisms, and given the fundamental chemical relatedness of DNA in all organisms, the source of the gene is of limited importance to judgments on safety. Rather, information on the gene product—the function of the protein that the gene encodes, its effect on the food and the way in which that food is intended to be used—all bear importantly on the safety of the food.

For example, many people are allergic to peanuts. If a gene from the peanut is transferred into a tomato, one might reasonably worry about the potential allergenicity of the tomato. However, if the protein encoded by that gene is known not to contribute to the allergenicity of peanuts, then the new tomato will not be a problem for people allergic to peanuts. Information about the source of the gene alone is thus of minimal usefulness.

The FDA's role

The FDA requires that the following questions be addressed before a food—genetically engineered or produced through traditional methods—is introduced to the marketplace:

- Does the food contain genes from known allergenic sources?
- Does it contain genes from toxigenic sources?
- Are the concentrations of natural toxigenic substances increased?
- Is the nutrient, fat or cholesterol content changed?
- Does the food contain a substance that is new to the food supply?

This policy, published in 1992, establishes that the FDA will treat as equivalent foods derived from plants modified by older breeding techniques and foods derived from plants modified by genetic engineering. The policy also introduces a new and conservative policy that establishes for the first time the principle that a genetic change in a plant adds something to food. Although the vast majority of foods from genetically modified plants will be considered equivalent to foods with a long history of safe use, certain foods will be subject to the food-additive provisions of the Food, Drug, and Cosmetic Act. A new substance may be considered a food additive, for example, if it is not substantially similar to substances with a history of safe use in the food supply.

Thus, under this policy, FDA will not ordinarily require premarket review if the food constituents from the new plant variety are the same or substantially similar to substances currently found in other foods. Premarket approval will be required when the characteristics of the new varieties raise safety questions or when substances in the new food are not considered substantially equivalent to those in common foods.

The genetic engineering of crops and food has been more carefully scrutinized . . . than any crop-breeding technology in the history of American agriculture.

Any food that contains a substance new to the food supply and that does not have a history of safe use would require premarket approval. Any food that contains increased levels of a natural toxicant would require approval and could be banned from the marketplace. The policy also addresses the potential for introducing an allergen into a food in which a consumer would not expect it. Foods derived from known allergenic sources must be demonstrated not to be allergenic or must be labeled to identify the source. In cases of potentially serious allergenicity risk, such foods would be banned from the food supply.

This approach has been supported by the American Medical Association and the American Dietetic Association.

Premarket testing should not be required

There are at least two reasons [to not require premarket testing]: cost and diminishing returns. Extensive testing adds costs to the food-production process. Those costs are passed on to consumers in the form of higher prices. Thus, most consumers will probably agree that extensive testing of the sort required under the Food Additive provisions of the Food, Drug, and Cosmetic Act should be limited to those new food products where there is a reason to believe a safety problem may exist or where the product is substantially different from any substance commonly used in the food supply.

The second reason, diminishing returns, stems from the fact that for some potential safety problems the most reliable tests are difficult and extremely expensive. Take allergenicity, for example. Only a very small percentage of the U.S. public has serious food allergies, and members of that group are allergic to different things. Thus, while it is true that for every food there is probably someone who is allergic to it, the number of people in the general population who are allergic to any one specific food is very small. For reasons of statistical accuracy, that means that each new food would have to be tested on a very large number of subjects to uncover the small subset who are sensitive to it.

This would not only be impractical on the scale of hundreds of new products introduced to consumers each year, but it would also be very expensive. The testing costs would drive up consumer prices. Of course, if the food that serves as the source of genetic material is known to be allergenic, such as peanuts or eggs, it can be tested on a much smaller group of individuals known to be sensitive.

Determining the safety of marker genes

Questions have been raised by the staff of the Environmental Defense Fund, an environmental advocacy group, about the safety of selectable marker genes in foods. The mere presence of a marker gene (or any other "foreign" DNA) or of the protein it encodes is not a genuine food-safety concern. [A marker gene is a gene that encodes an easily detected substance.] The pertinent issue is whether the gene product is safe. As consumers, we routinely ingest vast amounts of foreign, uncharacterized and largely extraneous genetic material (and encoded proteins) as a consequence of conventional plant breeding methods in all the fruits, nuts, vegetables and grains we eat every day. We have learned from this experience that new combinations of genes or entirely new kinds of genes or proteins in our foods are not, in and of themselves, indicators of risk.

Consider, as a case in point, the kanamycin resistance gene (used as a selectable marker in the production of Calgene's FlavrSavr® tomato). That same gene is found in harmless bacteria that are normally found on fresh fruits and vegetables. Many people would undoubtedly be surprised to learn that we routinely eat relatively large quantities of the bacteria, the gene and the gene product. The kanamycin resistance gene is also found in bacteria that populate the human gastrointestinal tract. In considering safety, it is no more or less relevant to know that the gene is used as a selectable marker in genetically engineered plants than it is to know that it is a normal component of bacteria that live on many of our foods or in our intestines. Safety is not determined by how or why the gene (and its product) was introduced into food—it is determined solely by the characteristics of the gene product and our experience with it in the food supply.

There is no merit to the argument that selectable marker genes, as a class of introduced genes, should be removed before genetically engineered foods enter the consumer marketplace. Their safety can be judged effectively by the same procedures and criteria articulated by the FDA policy for other introduced genes.

Labeling biotechnology foods

People are often apprehensive about change. Consumers may at first be concerned about new products, especially after prolonged, highly vocal controversy. When that concern is based on false claims or misconceptions of risk, however, it is better for government to meet it with accurate information.

Labeling is most useful when it provides reliable information that helps the consumer make substantive choices among products. Given that the label space available on any product is limited, the federal government has determined that food labels should be limited to information related to nutrition and health—information which would be of the greatest use to American consumers. With broad scientific consensus about the fundamental safety of the new genetic methods, the FDA has decided that the labeling of all biotechnology foods would provide consumers with no additional useful information on nutrition or healthfulness.

There is broad agreement that where claims of unique or heightened food safety risk are considered by regulators, they are best judged within the context of our experience with similar foods produced by conventional techniques. Scientific consensus does not support regulatory procedures that set all or most new biotechnology foods apart for special reporting requirements or labeling.

Consider one issue raised by a consumer organization. Consumers Union requested that the FDA require labeling for all genetically engineered foods from plant varieties with traits not commonly found in the breeding line from which that variety was derived. This request was not granted. Plant breeders, regulators and consumers have extensive experience with new grain, fruit and vegetable varieties created by cross breeding common crops with wild relatives that introduce traits never before expressed in those breeding lines. . . .

From this long history and from our experience with genetic engineering techniques, we can conclude that food safety is not a function of the "newness" of the genes and proteins introduced by breeding or genetic engineering. Safety is not a function of the genetic modification method—rDNA techniques do not change the fundamental biochemical rules of gene expression and protein synthesis.

Moreover, there is no reason to believe that products derived from conventional breeding or genetic engineering would be any more hazardous because they contained substances derived from other organisms. Extensive experience with such substances in medicine does not support the view that a protein derived from a different organism or one that is synthesized in a novel cellular environment is necessarily less safe or more likely to be allergenic.

Examples of widely and safely used products derived from other species—some exhibiting substantially different molecular composition from their human counterparts—include insulin derived from pig or cow; human interferon, streptokinase and TPA synthesized in bacteria or yeast; salmon calcitonin (30 percent of amino acid sequence different from human); and vaccines derived from infectious agents.

There is no logical reason for treating new biotechnology foods differently than other similar foods.

10
Agricultural Biotechnology Presents Health Risks

David Ehrenfeld

David Ehrenfeld is a professor of biology at Rutgers University in New Brunswick, New Jersey. He is the author of several books on biology and conservation, including Genes, Populations, and Species.

Agricultural biotechnology has undesirable health effects for people and animals. For example, cows treated with recombinant bovine growth hormone (rBGH) suffer side effects ranging from feeding disorders to mastitis, an udder infection that can lead to abnormal milk. Because these cows need more protein, they are often fed ground-up animals, which can lead to bovine spongiform encephalopathy (BSE), or "mad cow disease."As a result of rBGH and these feeding methods, humans are at greater risk for breast and gastro-intestinal cancers and Creutzfeldt-Jakob disease, which is analogous to BSE. The only beneficiaries of biotechnology are the chemical and seed companies who sell these products to farmers.

The modern history of agriculture has two faces. The first, a happy face, is turned toward non-farmers. It speaks brightly of technological miracles, such as the "Green Revolution" and, more recently, genetic engineering, that have resulted in the increased production of food for the world's hungry. The second face is turned toward the few remaining farmers who have survived these miracles. It is downcast and silent, like a mourner at a funeral.

The real purpose of biotechnology

The Green Revolution is an early instance of the co-opting of human needs by the techno-economic system. The latest manifestation of corporate agriculture is genetic engineering. Excluding military spending on fabulously expensive, dysfunctional weapons systems, there is no more dramatic case of people having their needs appropriated for the sake of

Reprinted from David Ehrenfeld, "A Cruel Agriculture," *Resurgence*, January/February 1998, with permission from both the author and *Resurgence*, Ford House, Hartland, Bideford, Devon EX39 6EE. Originally published as, "A Technopox upon the Land," in *Harper's Magazine*, October 1997, pp. 13–17.

profit at any cost. Like high-input agriculture, genetic engineering is often justified as a humane technology, one that feeds more people with better food. Nothing could be further from the truth. With very few exceptions, the whole point of genetic engineering is to increase the sales of chemicals and bio-engineered products to dependent farmers.

Social problems aside, this new agricultural biotechnology is on much shakier scientific ground than the Green Revolution ever was. Genetic engineering is based on the premise that we can take a gene from species A, where it does some desirable thing, and move it into species B, where it will continue to do that same desirable thing. Most genetic engineers know that this is not always true, but the biotech industry as a whole acts as if it were.

Genetic engineering is often justified as a humane technology, one that feeds more people with better food. Nothing could be further from the truth.

First, genes are not like tiny machines. The expression of their output can change when they are put in a new genetic and cellular environment. Second, genes usually have multiple effects. Undesirable effects that are suppressed in species A may be expressed when the gene is moved to species B. And third, many of the most important, genetically regulated traits that agricultural researchers deal with are controlled by multiple genes, perhaps on different chromosomes, and these are very resistant to manipulation by transgenic technology.

Because of these scientific limitations, agricultural biotechnology has been largely confined to applications that are basically simple-minded despite their technical complexity. Even here we find problems. The production of herbicide-resistant crop seeds is one example. Green Revolution crops tend to be on the wimpish side when it comes to competing with weeds—hence the heavy use of herbicides in recent decades. But many of the weeds are relatives of the crops, so the herbicides that kill the weeds can kill the crops too, given bad luck with weather and the timing of spraying. Enter the seed/chemical companies with a clever, profitable, unscrupulous idea. Why not introduce the gene for resistance to our own brand of herbicide into our own crop seeds, and then sell the patented seeds and patented herbicide as a package?

Never mind that this encourages farmers to apply recklessly large amounts of weedkiller, and that many herbicides have been associated with human sickness, including lymphoma. Nor that the genes for herbicide resistance can move naturally from the crops to the related weeds via pollen transfer, rendering the herbicide ineffective in a few years. What matters, as an agricultural biotechnologist once remarked to me, is earning enough profit to keep the company happy.

A related agricultural biotechnology is the transfer of bacterial or plant genes that produce a natural insecticide directly into crops such as corn and cotton. An example is Bt (*Bacillus thuringiensis*), which has been widely used as an external dust or spray to kill harmful beetles and moths. In this traditional use, Bt breaks down into harmless components in a day or two, and the surviving pests do not get a chance to evolve resistance to it. But with Bt now produced continuously inside genetically engineered crops, which are planted over hundreds of thousands of acres, the emergence of genetic resistance among the pests becomes almost a certainty.

Monsanto, one of the world's largest manufacturers of agricultural chemicals, has patented cottonseed containing genes for Bt. Advertised as being effective against bollworms without the use of additional insecticides, 1,800,000 acres in five southern states of the USA were planted with this transgenic seed in 1996, at a cost to farmers of not only the seed itself but an additional $32-per-acre "technology fee" paid to Monsanto. Heavy bollworm infestation occurred in spite of the special seed, forcing farmers to spray expensive insecticides anyway. Those farmers who wanted to use seeds from the surviving crop to replace the damaged crop found that Monsanto's licensing agreement, like most others in the industry, permitted them only one planting.

Troubles with Monsanto's genetically engineered seed have not been confined to cotton. In May 1997, Monsanto Canada and its licensee, Limagrain Canada Seeds, recalled 60,000 bags of "Roundup-ready" canola seeds because they mistakenly contained a gene that had not been tested by the government for human consumption. These seeds, engineered to resist Monsanto's most profitable product, the herbicide Roundup, were enough to plant more than 600,000 acres. Two farmers had already planted the seeds when Monsanto discovered its mistake.

Dangerous genetic tampering

There is another shaky scientific premise of agricultural biotechnology. This concerns the transfer of animal or plant genes from the parent species into micro-organisms, so that the valuable products of these genes can then be produced in large commercial batches. The assumption here is that these transgenic products, when administered back to the parent species in large doses, will simply increase whatever desirable effect they normally have. Again, this is simplistic thinking that totally ignores the great complexity of living organisms and the consequences of tampering with them.

In the United States, one of the most widely deployed instances of this sort of biotechnology is the use of recombinant bovine growth hormone (rBGH), which is produced by placing slightly modified cow genes into fermentation tanks containing bacteria, then injected into lactating cows to make them yield more milk. This is done despite our nationwide milk glut and despite the fact that the use of rBGH will probably accelerate the demise of the small dairy farm, since only large farms are able to take on the extra debt for the more expensive feeds, the high-tech feed-management systems, and the added veterinary care that go along with its use.

The side effects of rBGH on cows are also serious. Recombinant BGH-related problems—as stated on the package insert by its manufacturer, Monsanto—include bloat, diarrhoea, diseases of the knees and feet, feeding disorders, fevers, reduced blood haemoglobin levels, cystic ovaries, uterine pathology, reduced pregnancy rates, smaller calves, and mastitis—an udder infection that can result, according to the insert, in "visibly abnormal milk". Treatment of mastitis can lead to the presence of antibiotics in milk, probably accelerating the spread of antibiotic resistance among bacteria that cause human disease. Milk from rBGH-treated cows may also contain insulin growth factor, IGF-1, which has been implicated in human breast and gastro-intestinal cancers.

Another potential problem is an indirect side-effect of the special nutritional requirements of rBGH-treated cows. Because these cows require more protein, their feed is supplemented with ground-up animals, a practice that has been associated with bovine spongiform encephalopathy (BSE), also known as "mad cow disease". The recent British epidemic of BSE appears to have been associated with an increased incidence of the disease's human analogue, Creutzfeldt-Jakob disease. There seems little reason to increase the risk of this terrible disease for the sake of a biotechnology that we don't need. If cows stay off hormones and concentrate on eating grass, all of us will be much better off.

Meanwhile the biotechnology juggernaut rolls on, converting humanity's collective agricultural heritage from an enduring, farmer-controlled lifestyle to an energy-dependent, corporate "process". The ultimate co-optation is the patenting of life. The Supreme Court's ruling in the case of *Diamond* v. *Chakrabarty* in 1980 paved the way for corporations to obtain industrial, or "utility", patents on living organisms, from bacteria to human cells. These patents operate like the patents on mechanical inventions, granting the patent-holder a more sweeping and longer-lasting control than had been conferred by the older forms of plant patents.

Somehow, in the chaos of technological change, we have lost the distinction between a person and a corporation, inexplicably valuing profit at any cost over basic human needs. In doing so we have forsaken our farmers, the spiritual descendants of those early Hebrew and Greek farmers and pastoralists who first gave us our understanding of social justice, democracy, and the existence of a power greater than our own. No amount of lip-service to the goal of feeding the world's hungry or to the glory of a new technology, and no amount of transient increases in the world's grain production, can hide this terrible truth.

11

The Government and Private Sector Should Work Together to Improve Food Safety

Catherine Woteki

Catherine Woteki is the under secretary for food safety at the U.S. Department of Agriculture.

The federal, state, and local governments, along with the private sector, need to work together to ensure the continued safety of America's food supply. The different levels of government can improve food safety by integrating their resources and focusing on specific roles, such as identifying food hazards or regulating the retail food sector. The private sector can play an important part in research and education.

Editor's Note: The following viewpoint was originally a speech given at the Food Industry Conference hosted by Pennsylvania State University in Grantville, Pennsylvania, on March 31, 1999.

It's a pleasure to be here to talk about integrating resources to improve food safety. The fact that you are holding this conference on strengthening partnerships shows that you have already gotten the message of how important it is for all of us—government, industry, academia, and consumers—to work together to improve food safety.

Over the past several years, I believe we have made a lot of progress in establishing a framework that has been used, and will continue to be used, to make significant improvements in food safety. By a framework, I mean that we have identified distinct areas where we know progress is needed. This framework was presented in its entirety to the public in May 1997 as the President's Food Safety Initiative. In that document, seven

Reprinted from Catherine Woteki's speech, "Integrating Resources to Improve Food Safety," to the Food Industry Conference, March 31, 1999; available at http://www.fsis.usda.gov/OA/speeches/cw_penn.htm.

key areas were outlined: foodborne disease surveillance, outbreak response, risk assessment, research, inspections, education, and strategic
planning. While progress in some of these areas has been more rapid than
in others, all are essential to our goal of reducing the incidence of foodborne illness.

We knew, when this framework was developed, that identifying areas
where progress is needed was only the beginning. It would take a lot of
work, and good coordination, among the various public and private organizations responsible for food safety. Now that the framework is in
place, and we know *what* to do, I believe we are seeing an increasing focus on *how* we are going to get the job done. By "we," I mean the collective we. How are we going to integrate resources to improve food safety?
Specifically, how are the federal agencies responsible for food safety going
to work together? How can federal agencies work most effectively with
state and local governments? How can government best work with industry, academia, and others involved in food safety? These are questions
we need to answer.

Some food safety recommendations

These questions are particularly timely because of recent questions raised
about whether federal food safety activities are organized in a manner
that promotes the greatest progress. On August 20, 1998, the National
Academy of Sciences released its report, "Ensuring Safe Food from Production to Consumption." This study was begun in 1998 at the request
of Congress to determine the scientific and organizational needs of an effective federal food safety system.

Shortly afterward, on August 25, President Clinton created his Food
Safety Council, which he charged with developing a comprehensive
strategic plan for federal food safety activities and ensuring that federal
agencies develop coordinated food safety budgets each year. One of the
Council's first jobs was to review the Academy's study, solicit public in-
put, and report back to the President with recommendations on appropriate actions to improve food safety. The response, which was released
on March 15, 1999, supports all of the goals contained in the Academy's
recommendations to strengthen the food safety system.

The Council responded to each of the recommendations in the Academy's report with the following specific assessments.

---

*Federal, state, and local governments have distinct
roles when it comes to food safety.*

Recommendation 1 was that the food safety system should be based
on science. The Council agreed and provided numerous examples of
where this is already the case, including the development and implementation of the FoodNet and PulseNet systems for surveillance and
identification of foodborne pathogens, and the implementation of new
science-based inspections of meat, poultry, and seafood. The Council has
identified areas that should be strengthened, such as improving the abil-

ity to assess health risks from pathogens in food.

Recommendation 2 was that federal statutes should be based on scientifically supportable risks to public health. The Council agrees and will call on Congress to work with it to create scientifically-based statutes to promote food safety. The Council will conduct a thorough review of existing statutes and determine what can be accomplished with existing regulatory flexibility and what improvements will require statutory changes.

Recommendation 3 was that a comprehensive national food safety plan should be developed. The development of such a plan is already underway and is one of the primary functions of the Council. One component of the plan will be exploring methods to assess the comparative health risks of the nation's food supply.

Recommendation 4 was that a new statute should be enacted that establishes a unified framework for food safety programs with a single official having control over all federal food safety resources. The Council supports the goal of a unified framework for food safety programs and will conduct an assessment of structural models and other mechanisms to strengthen the federal food safety system through better coordination, planning and resource allocation.

Recommendation 5 was that agencies should work more effectively with partners in state and local governments. The Council agrees that the roles of state, tribal, and local governments in the food safety system are critical and that their efforts deserve the formal recognition that partnership in a national food safety system conveys.

The government's role

I'd like to talk in more detail about this last recommendation, because it emphasizes that a national food safety system must involve state and local governments as well. Our goal is the integration of federal, state, and local government activities toward a common food safety goal. But what exactly does this mean?

First, I believe it means acknowledging that the federal, state, and local governments have distinct roles when it comes to food safety. For example, the federal government, I believe, should take the lead, with academia, in the identification of food hazards through risk assessment. It also should be responsible for establishing food safety standards that can then be applied jointly by federal and state programs. And the federal government should take the lead in encouraging national and international uniformity in food safety standards in order to maintain consumer confidence in the safety of food, regardless of whether it was produced under a state, federal, or foreign inspection program.

The states, on the other hand, have the lead regulatory role over the retail food sector, with support from FDA, U.S. Department of Agriculture (USDA), and others. This is an increasingly important area of public concern, as we find the distinction between retail and inspected establishments blurring, with many retail operations now carrying out the same processing operations. We also recognize the state's primary role in animal production food safety. The states already have networks in place to address this segment of the farm-to-table chain.

Integrating federal, state, and local resources also means sharing information. New scientific developments mean that more data are being generated on foodborne illness and on the prevalence of pathogens in foods. We also have valuable information from research carried out by both the public and private sectors. We need to share this information on a regular basis.

At the federal level, Food Safety and Inspection Service (FSIS) and FDA recently signed a memorandum of understanding (MOU) to facilitate the exchange of information at the field level about food establishments under shared jurisdiction. The MOU establishes procedures for notifying each other in the event one agency discovers contaminated foods that are an imminent health hazard, for example, or when either of us takes an enforcement action. It's a small step, but it is an example of the direction in which we are headed.

Another way we are sharing information is through a series of training sessions for state and local food inspection officials on the potential health risks associated with meat and poultry products processed at the retail level and in food service operations. We are working with the Association of Food and Drug Officials on this important initiative.

Integrating resources at the federal, state, and local levels also means working collaboratively on projects involving food safety. As a result of the President's Food Safety Initiative, we have seen a number of collaborative projects at the federal and state level already.

For example, we have the Foodborne Outbreak Response Coordinating Group—FORCEG—the intergovernmental group of federal and state agencies formed to improve responses to interstate outbreaks of foodborne illness. The FoodNet active surveillance network for foodborne disease also involves all levels of government.

USDA strongly believes that in order to integrate resources, the federal government must do what it can to strengthen our state partnerships, and I believe our commitment is quite evident.

In the area of inspection, we have provided extensive technical assistance to more than 2,800 small plants to help them meet the requirements of the Pathogen Reduction and Hazard Analysis and Critical Control Point (HACCP) rule. We are now beginning an assistance program for very small plants, which must implement the requirements by January 2000. I want to take a moment to thank Pennsylvania State University for its assistance in helping us with this initiative. Penn State is one of several universities that have volunteered to implement HACCP in its meat and poultry pilot plant so that very small plants can see HACCP in action.

Public-private partnerships are critical to meeting our food safety goals.

Under the fiscal year 2000 budget request for FSIS, further progress can be made in strengthening state partnerships. For example, under the Food Safety Initiative, $2.4 million is earmarked to help the states comply with the Pathogen Reduction and HACCP requirements, which is a major prerequisite for permitting the interstate shipment of state-inspected products. And $0.5 million is earmarked to improve emergency response coordination with the states in investigating foodborne disease outbreaks. During FY2000, FSIS also intends to continue its assistance to the states to help them automate their systems. And FSIS is seeking cooperative agreement authority, which would allow it to enter into partnerships with organizations such as state and federal government agencies, academia, and industry. Currently, FSIS must work through other federal agencies to enter into cooperative agreements, and must pay additional costs for this service.

Since 1995, USDA and the Department of Health and Human Services have together held several meetings to explore how federal, state, and local agencies can arrive at a national, seamless food safety system, and we can expect such meetings to continue. In February 1999, FSIS hosted a National Food Safety Conference for senior food safety officials in each state. Out of these meetings, a National Integrated Food Safety System Project, involving federal, state, and local officials, has been established, and we expect to see good ideas emerge from this effort.

Public-private partnerships

I don't want to leave the private sector out of this discussion, because public-private partnerships are critical to meeting our food safety goals. The President's Food Safety Initiative places a heavy emphasis on public and private partnerships, and we are seeing progress on this front as well.

The Fight BAC! campaign, the result of the public-private Partnership for Food Safety Education, is spreading the word to consumers about taking basic sanitation and food handling steps to protect themselves from foodborne illness. And the education of food handlers in food service operations and at the retail level is being addressed by the Food Safety Training and Education Alliance—which includes representatives from industry and consumer groups, trade associations, and government agencies.

Research is another area where the private sector plays an important role. We need a strong research base so that we have the best science on which to base policy decisions. We also need research to develop interventions that can be used farm-to-table to improve food safety.

The federal government plays a large role in supporting food safety research, and in July 1998, President Clinton announced the creation of the Joint Institute for Food Safety Research. The Institute is charged with developing a strategic plan for conducting food safety research and coordinating all federal food safety research—including research conducted with the private sector and academia.

The private sector's involvement in improving the research base is critical, and fortunately, we are seeing positive developments. There are a growing number of public-private partnerships, such as the Joint Institute for Food Safety and Applied Nutrition (JIFSAN), which is a collaborative activity of FDA and the University of Maryland, and the Illinois Institute of Technology's Moffet Center in Chicago, which is partially supported by the food industry. And USDA's Agricultural Research Service has, for more than a decade, used Cooperative Research and Development Agreements, under which USDA scientists develop a technology, and a private company receives the licensing rights. This arrangement was used to create PREEMPT—a product that significantly reduces *Salmonella* contamination in chickens. And we are seeing industry take the initiative to fund research on its own. The National Cattlemen's Beef Association, for example, announced its commitment to implementing a $40 million research plan to further pathogen reduction.

Bipartisan support for food safety

Food safety has emerged in recent years as a major area of consumer concern and a major area of congressional concern. Widespread media reports of massive contaminated food product recalls and of foodborne illness outbreaks perhaps have contributed to a public perception that the nation's food supply may be less safe today than it was only a few decades ago.

On one hand, that perception is not altogether accurate. While we may be reading and hearing more about contaminated products and about people who get sick from eating those products, we should not conclude that today's food marketplace poses a significantly greater risk to public health. In a world of high technology and rapid, mass communications, we simply are more readily able in the 1990s to identify links between contaminated products and foodborne illnesses and quickly alert consumers, largely through mass media. I believe the U.S. food supply remains one of the safest, if not the safest, in the world.

On the other hand, we have plenty of reasons to remain highly conscious of food supply threats. Today's food production and delivery system is vastly different from yesterday's. Food comes from all over the world. It is produced in mass quantities and often shipped great distances in relatively short times. Food is sold and prepared and cooked in a variety of ways and under a variety of circumstances. In a more fast-paced world, Americans rely more than ever before on food that can be quickly obtained, prepared, and eaten. Add emerging new pathogens and persistent old ones to the changing consumption habits of today's American, and you have a food supply that is not unsafe, but that is vulnerable.

As Under Secretary for the USDA agency that oversees inspection of the nation's meat and poultry and egg products, I am encouraged by our progress in preventing contaminated food products from reaching the marketplace. Our science-based and prevention-oriented inspection system called Hazard Analysis and Critical Control Point (HACCP) Systems is being implemented in processing plants across the country over a three-year period that began in January 1998. Results from phase one indicate it is helping to reduce product contamination and foodborne illnesses.

> *I believe the U.S. food supply remains one of the safest, if not the safest, in the world.*

The President's Food Safety Initiative, which is proposed for its third consecutive funding year in fiscal year 2000, also has contributed to a safer food supply by providing funding for food safety research and education, foodborne illness surveillance and coordination, inspection, and other activities critical to public health. We are making great progress in the war on unsafe food.

In the past, we have been fortunate to have bipartisan support for our food safety initiatives and appropriate levels of funding to maintain our skilled inspection workforce. By law, our workforce must oversee the slaughter and processing of meat and poultry products and the processing of egg products and verify that industry is meeting its food safety responsibilities. It is essential that the levels of funding proposed by the President be maintained for our inspection force to do its job of protecting the domestic and international meat and poultry supply. Unfortunately, there is some concern that proposals for across the board cuts could diminish our ability to provide that important inspection. Such a cut would have a devastating effect on the safety of those products we inspect.

As I mentioned, food safety enjoys strong bipartisan support, and it is not my intent here to evaluate competing budgets—except when it comes to food safety and public health.

In closing, the importance of integrating our resources and working in a coordinated fashion is without question.

Despite the fact that we focus on different commodities and address different parts of the farm-to-table chain, food safety is a common goal that ties us together.

I look forward to working with you as we make further progress on creating a seamless, national food safety system and on making the food supply as safe as it can possibly be.

12

The Private Sector Can Ensure Food Safety

E.C. Pasour Jr.

E.C. Pasour Jr. is a professor emeritus at North Carolina State University, at the College of Agriculture and Life Sciences.

The private sector, particularly the meat industry, is better equipped than the government to inspect food. Consumers should not rely on the government to ensure food safety because its regulations are often flawed and ineffective. Market regulation is a superior option, since it provides a financial incentive to private inspection firms and meat companies. If a private firm conducts ineffective inspections, or a meat producer sells contaminated meat, that company will suffer financially. Firms are thus encouraged to ensure the production and sale of safe meat in order to attract customers.

Nineteen-ninety-seven's news reports of tainted beef focused public attention on the safety of the meat supply. In August 1997, Secretary of Agriculture Dan Glickman forced Hudson Foods to recall 25 million pounds of hamburger meat produced at the firm's state-of-the-art plant in Nebraska. The nation's largest beef recall occurred after several Colorado consumers became sick from hamburgers linked to E. coli contamination.

Examples of illness rooted in unsafe meat are not isolated incidents. Bad or undercooked meat causes an estimated 4,000 deaths and 5 million illnesses annually, according to the federal government's Centers for Disease Control.[1] Moreover, a single incident of contaminated meat has the potential to affect large numbers of people. In 1993, five hundred people became ill and four children died in the Pacific northwest as a result of eating tainted hamburgers.

Overreliance on government regulations

Illness and death caused by bad meat (whether tainted or undercooked) inevitably evoke calls for more government regulation. It is ironic that increased government intervention is viewed as an antidote to tainted

Reprinted from E.C. Pasour Jr., "We Can Do Better than Government Inspection of Meat," *The Freeman*, May 1998, with permission from the publisher.

meat, despite the federal government's long-standing responsibility for meat inspection in the United States. Indeed, the Hudson Foods incident occurred only a year after President Bill Clinton announced the most sweeping changes in the government's meat-inspection system. Moreover, a federal inspector was based at the Hudson Foods plant to check the plant's procedures daily.

Chronic problems related to meat inspection and meat safety warrant increased scrutiny of the most appropriate method of inspecting meat. During recent decades, successful deregulation initiatives occurred in a number of areas including banking and transportation. This shows that market forces may provide an improvement over government regulation of economic activity, even when regulations are long-standing and widely accepted.

Skeptics, including even many market proponents, might say that the conventional analysis doesn't hold for government regulations protecting health—where slip-ups can be fatal. Problems of "government failure" however, may be worse than any market imperfections that government regulation is instituted to remedy.[2] Thus, government failure would have even graver implications for health issues.

Is it possible that the free market could substitute for, and even improve on, the current system of federal meat inspection? The following analysis demonstrates that the problems in government meat inspection are similar to those that plague all other government regulation of economic activity. There is no way for government regulators to obtain the information and realize the incentives of the decentralized market process, whatever the area of economic activity. Thus, market inspection of the U.S. meat industry, when contrasted with the current system of federal regulation, is likely to reduce the incidence of illness associated with the consumption of unsafe meat.

The history of meat inspection

The Meat Inspection Act of 1891 was a major landmark in federal regulation of meat and, indeed, of federal regulation of economic activity in the United States.[3] A review of the political economy of that era is helpful in understanding the impetus for government regulation. Most government intervention then and now, at least ostensibly, is in response to "market failure"—economic outcomes that fall short of "perfect competition." (All markets fail, of course, when measured against this criterion.)

Moreover, the 1891 act was instituted under false pretenses. It was a solution to a largely nonexistent problem—contaminated meat. There is no reliable evidence that tainted meat was a major factor in the adoption of the legislation. In a political-economic analysis of the era, Gary Libecap concludes that "the record does not indicate that the incidence of diseased cattle or their consumption was very great, and there is no evidence of a major health issue at that time over beef consumption."[4] Government meat inspection, once in place, however, like many other government regulations, was soon viewed as necessary to protect consumers.

There is a great deal of evidence that the political impetus for the 1891 legislation was the consequence of rapidly changing economic conditions. Market dominance by Chicago meat-packers—primarily Swift,

Armour, Morris, and Hammond—quickly followed the introduction of refrigeration around 1880. Refrigeration allowed for centralized, large-scale, and lower-cost slaughterhouses because of production, distribution, and transportation advantages. The four large Chicago firms accounted for about 90 percent of the cattle slaughtered in Chicago within a decade after the introduction of refrigeration.

The problems in government meat inspection are similar to those that plague all other government regulation of economic activity.

The Chicago packers fundamentally changed demand and supply conditions in the meatpacking industry. Small, local slaughterhouses throughout the country were rapidly displaced because they could not compete with the lower-cost Chicago packers. Local slaughter firms, in response, charged that Chicago packers used diseased cattle and that their dressed beef was unsafe. The disease issue, as bogus as it apparently was, threatened both domestic demand and export markets for U.S. meat. Cattle raisers, especially those in the midwest, backed federal meat inspection to promote demand.[5]

Cattle producers were also concerned about falling prices. Prices fell because the supply of cattle grew rapidly. But producers attributed the fall to their declining market power versus the Chicago packers—a charge that seemed credible because of the packers' size and concentration. Ostensibly to deal with the largely spurious allegations of unsafe meat and collusion by the Chicago packers, cattlemen, and local packers called for federal meat inspection and antitrust legislation. Enactment of the Sherman Act in 1890 and the Meat Inspection Act of 1891 were thus closely tied legislatively.[6]

The famous Meat Inspection Act of 1906 also was heavily influenced by false charges. Ideas have consequences, and public policy can be influenced by a popular book, such as Upton Sinclair's *The Jungle*—regardless of its merits. The muckraking novel focused on greed and abuse among Chicago meat-packers and government inspectors.[7] The characters in *The Jungle* tell of workers falling into tanks, being ground up with animal parts, and being made into "Durham's Pure Leaf Lard."

Sinclair wrote *The Jungle* to ignite a socialist movement on behalf of America's workers. He did not even pretend to have actually witnessed or verified the horrendous conditions he ascribed to Chicago packing houses. Instead, he relied heavily on both his own imagination and hearsay. Indeed, a congressional investigation at the time found little substance in Sinclair's allegations.[8]

Nevertheless, the sensational allegations dramatically reduced the demand for meat. U.S. exports fell by half. Major meat-packers saw new regulations as the way to restore confidence, and they strongly endorsed the Meat Inspection Act of 1906, which expanded the scope of federal inspection to include smaller competitors.

Economic conditions back then were much different from today's. However, there is a lesson to be learned from that early period concerning government and free-market approaches to meat inspection.

The early legislation, for the most part, was not a response by government to a legitimate public-health threat. Congress enacted the 1891 act in response to political pressure by local meat-packers and cattle growers who felt victimized by the rise in power of the Chicago packers and by lower cattle prices. This legislation along with the Sherman Act and the Interstate Commerce Act, all enacted within a four-year period, represented a significant break with what had previously been considered an appropriate role for the federal government.[9]

The 1906 Meat Inspection Act, too, was largely a response to the meat industry's financial problems rather than to a health threat. The earlier spate of interventionist legislation, however, had provided a new mandate for government regulation of economic activity that facilitated the passage of the 1906 act. Thus, the case of federal meat inspection is yet another example of Ludwig von Mises's insight that government intervention almost inevitably leads to further intervention.

Pitfalls of government regulation

Thus government meat inspection, like most other economic regulation, was instituted mainly because of favor-seeking: the use of time and money to harness the power of government for private ends.[10] Favor-seeking is a negative-sum activity. The nation's output of goods and services decreases as resources are used to restrict competition rather than to expand production and exchange. Favor-seeking is just one example of "government failure."

Government intervention often is counterproductive because of information and incentive problems. The crucial economic problem confronting society is how to use people's specialized knowledge to best satisfy consumers. As Nobel laureate F.A. Hayek emphasized, government officials cannot obtain the information that motivates individual choice because that information, much of which is never articulated, is strongly linked to a particular time and place. Consequently, officials must base decisions on something other than the "public interest," if that term means the interests of the people who comprise the public.

Moreover, even if the information could be known, it is unlikely to be used most effectively. Government officials lack appropriate incentives because power and responsibility are separated. Those who make and administer laws do not bear the consequences of their actions, at least not to the same extent as private individuals. As shown below, markets generally are superior to government regulation because they cope better with information and incentive problems.

Related to the incentive problem is another flaw in the current system of meat inspection: the adverse effect of government regulation on innovation. That flaw is found in all alternatives to the decentralized market process.[11]

In the absence of the profit motive, individuals have less incentive to discover and implement new technology in the inspection and handling of meat. No one knows, of course, which new technology will ultimately prove beneficial in meat inspection or in any other area. However, in the marketplace, if an innovation proves to be profitable the person responsible for it will receive a large part of the reward. Things are quite different in a centralized system. Under government regulation, the government employee who discovers or adopts a potentially superior technology is likely to receive only a small amount of additional compensation. On the other hand, if the innovation doesn't pan out, he will lose much less than the entrepreneur in a profit-and-loss system.

Government regulation gives consumers a false sense of security.

This fundamental difference between markets and government is highly important to innovation in the meat industry. The heart of U.S. meat inspection continues to be the "poke and sniff" method that relies on the eyes and noses of some 7,400 Department of Agriculture inspectors. In 1997 a small Massachusetts company, SatCon Technology Corporation, working with a North Dakota–based group of ranchers, found a way to use lasers to find illness-causing pathogens such as E. coli and salmonella by scanning animal carcasses in slaughterhouses.[12] Such technological innovation has the potential to revolutionize meat inspection in the United States.

But it is more likely to be adopted in a free market than in a government-regulated market. Since it has the potential to dramatically reduce both the amount of labor currently used in meat inspection and the rationale for government regulation, it is inconsistent with two important goals of any bureaucracy: maintaining jobs and expanding its operation.

The advantages of private inspection

The experience of government control of economic activity shows why government meat inspection is likely to be inferior to free markets. Private inspection firms, which must meet the market test, have a greater incentive to be effective than do government regulators. A private firm providing information to consumers about meat quality will reap profits when successful and incur losses when not. Thus, if a private meat-grading service were to become lax in satisfying consumers, meat firms no longer would be willing to pay for the service. Consequently, the private firm not only has an advantage in obtaining the necessary information; it also has a greater incentive to use it in the interest of the public weal.

Moreover, profit-seeking firms are likely to have a greater incentive than government regulators to adhere to quality standards. Government inspectors get to know the people operating the plants they regulate. Strict enforcement of standards might create hardship for those people. For example, if meat is considered to be of marginal quality but not to pose a significant health threat, regulators may be inclined to overlook such infractions. In short, when contrasted with market regulation, government regulators have a smaller incentive to enforce safety regulations.

Numerous studies have shown the benefits from privatization. It is quite likely that problems of food safety would be dealt with better through the decentralized market process, which provides a greater opportunity for both business firms and consumers to achieve their goals. Stated differently, the market process provides a greater incentive than government regulation for private firms and consumers to discover, disseminate, and use information about the quality of meat.

For one thing, government regulation gives consumers a false sense of security.[13] It leads them to assume that they are being protected by the government, reducing the incentive to do their own checking. Market methods of inspection, in contrast, give consumers a greater incentive to acquire information about the quality of meat. Consequently, they are likely to be more alert to potential problems of food safety.

It is true, of course, that meat may be contaminated when it appears to be safe. If sellers of meat have more information about quality than consumers do, can consumers look after their interests? Yes; uneven information does not imply that sellers have an incentive to sell unsafe meat. Consumers are protected by the sellers' economic interests.

The use of brand names, such as Armour or Swift, is one way that private firms assure quality standards for meat.[14] A brand name enables consumers to identify a firm's meat product and choose it over competitors. Hence, a firm with an established and valuable brand name has a strong financial incentive to adhere to quality standards.

A company responsible for selling contaminated meat can be quickly ruined by adverse publicity about its products. The recall of Hudson beef in 1997 left Burger King branches across the midwest without hamburgers. Following the recall, Burger King canceled their contract with Hudson Foods and announced that it would never buy from the company again— showing that it is strongly in the financial interest of business firms not to sell tainted meat.

Where quality is difficult for consumers to evaluate, little-known firms may benefit from the services of private inspectors to certify safety. There is considerable evidence that market forces can assure product quality without government regulation. Best Western, for example, is a private certification agency that enables travelers to identify motels that meet specified quality standards. Underwriters Laboratories establishes standards for electrical products, and tests them to see if they meet those standards. These examples show that firms frequently are willing to pay to assure customers that their products meet prescribed standards. The success of *Consumer Reports* and similar publications is further evidence that consumers are willing to pay to be informed.

Businesses and consumers are willing to pay to assure product quality.

Is meat inspection an exception to the rule that private firms generally perform more effectively than government? There are good reasons to think that market-based inspection of the meat industry could improve on the current system. Illness associated with contaminated meat often occurs with federal meat inspection. There is no way, of course, to prevent all food-related illness. Mistakes on the part of buyers and sellers, and some degree of fraud, are unavoidable whatever the institutional arrangement. The goal in meat inspection, as in other areas of economic activity, is to establish an institutional arrangement that provides and uses information in a way that best serves consumers. The free market generally is more effective than government regulation in doing so.

Market regulation should be encouraged

We've seen that businesses and consumers are willing to pay to assure product quality. And, as emphasized throughout, it is apparent that private inspection agencies "have a lot going for them."[15] Yet, despite the ostensible advantages of the market approach, there is little reliance on market forces in meat inspection in the United States. Why does the meat industry not rely on market regulation more?

Market-generated information about the quality of meat undoubtedly would be much greater in the absence of government regulation. Government inspection tends to preempt market inspection, much as taxpayer-financed education crowds out privately funded schools, by reducing the incentives of sellers and buyers to look after safety on their own.[16] There is little demand on the part of meat handlers for services that would be provided by private firms in the absence of government inspection. Business firms are, of course, also happy to have the taxpayers pick up the tab for inspection.

Similarly, with assurances by the U.S. Department of Agriculture (USDA) (and the media) that government regulation is crucial to consumer safety, there is little impetus for consumers to change the current institutional arrangement. Moreover, when problems of meat safety occur, there is no discussion of "government failure." Instead, regulatory officials plead for more power. In the aftermath of the Hudson Foods incident, for example, Secretary Glickman requested additional authority to shut down food-processing plants and to impose fines of $100,000 per day on any plant not obeying his order.

There can be no guarantees when it comes to food safety. Indeed, zero risk is not a reasonable objective in any aspect of human action. There are two approaches to ensuring the safety of meat—market inspection and government regulation. It is ironic that the public expects government regulation, which has more imperfections than the competitive market process, to provide for meat safety.[17] Few people question the appropriateness of government regulation of the meat industry, even when they fault its effectiveness.

No one has a stronger interest in protecting consumers from tainted meat than the businesses in the industry. Ultimately, safety is best assured when rooted in the self-interest of business firms and consumers.

Notes

1. Peter J. Howe, "New Laser May Identify Tainted Meat," *The Boston Globe*, 1997, http://yourhealthdaily.com/090497_110006_15810.html.

2. William C. Mitchell and Randy T. Simmons, *Beyond Politics: Markets, Welfare, and the Failure of Bureaucracy* (Boulder, Colo.: Westview Press, 1994).

3. Information presented here on the early history of meat inspection in the United States relies heavily on Gary D. Libecap, "The Rise of the Chicago

Packers, and the Origins of Meat Inspection and Antitrust," *Economic Inquiry*, April 1992, pp. 242–62.

4. Ibid., p. 246.

5. Ibid., p. 244.

6. Ibid.

7. Lawrence W. Reed, "Of Meat and Myth," *The Freeman*, November 1994, pp. 600–02.

8. Ibid., pp. 600–01.

9. Libecap, p. 242.

10. Economists use the term "rent-seeking." James D. Gwartney and Richard L. Stroup, *Economics: Private and Public Choice*, 8th ed. (Orlando, Fla.: Harcourt Brace & Co., 1997), p. 102.

11. Milton Friedman, *Market Mechanisms and Central Economic Planning* (Washington, D.C.: American Enterprise Institute for Public Policy Research, 1981), p. 21.

12. Howe.

13. Randall G. Holcombe, *Public Policy and the Quality of Life: Market Imperfections Versus Government Planning* (Westport, Conn.: Greenwood Press, 1995), p. 105.

14. The discussion of quality standards draws on Holcombe, pp. 93–106.

15. Ibid., p. 101.

16. E.C. Pasour, Jr., "Consumer Information and the Calculation Debate," *The Freeman*, December 1996, pp. 780–86.

17. Mitchell and Simmons, p. 82.

13

Food-Disparagement Laws May Not Reduce Food Safety Scares

Kenneth Smith

Kenneth Smith is an editorial writer for the Washington Times.

Food-disparagement laws will probably not reduce the food safety scares propagated by the television shows such as *Oprah Winfrey* and *60 Minutes*. These laws, which have been passed in thirteen states, make it illegal for people to knowingly spread misinformation about perishable foods. However, food producers are not likely to win these suits, even if the disparagements are wildly inaccurate.

"Let me warn you, today's show may cause you to diet for all the wrong reasons. We're talking about the hidden dangers in our food, possibly the food in your own refrigerator. . . . [I]t's the biggest health scare to hit Europe since the Chernobyl nuclear disaster. Mad cow disease has stunned the world." So announced Oprah Winfrey on "Dangerous Food," the April 16, 1996, edition of *The Oprah Winfrey Show*. After drawing attention to two victims of the human equivalent of "mad cow disease" (BSE),[1] who allegedly had contracted it by eating contaminated beef, she asked Howard Lyman of the Humane Society: "You say this disease could make AIDS look like the common cold?" "Absolutely," Lyman answered. Before the program ended, Ms. Winfrey herself had sworn off eating both chicken and beef. "It has just stopped me cold from eating another burger," she said.

Food-disparagement lawsuits

Not long afterward, many people followed suit. Cattle prices fell to 10-year lows, devastating farmers—who subsequently sued Ms. Winfrey, her production company, and the Humane Society's Lyman for $6.7 million in damages. The farmers didn't, however, sue under the usual laws de-

Reprinted from Kenneth Smith, "'Let Me Warn You . . .': Oprah, the Law, and Bad-Mouthing Foods," *Priorities*, vol. 10, no. 1, 1998, with permission from the American Council on Science & Health.

signed to protect people against libel: The Texas Beef Group and other feed and cattle organizations sued under a state statute that makes knowingly spreading misinformation about the safety of a perishable food product illegal. Critics dismiss such statutes as "veggie libel" laws or "banana bills," yet regard them as serious threats to free speech. They could, for example, restrain debate over worthy food-safety issues. [Winfrey won the suit in February 1998. The case was appealed but no decision had been reached as of May 1999.]

Proponents of food-disparagement statutes wave off such concerns. Steve Kopperud, Senior Vice President of the American Feed Industry Association, notes that he was a reporter for 15 years and that the last thing he wants is to muzzle the press or destroy the First Amendment. "But if activists stand up and say, 'Cauliflower causes breast cancer,' they've got to be able to prove that," he told a reporter for Knight-Ridder newspapers. "I think that to the degree that the mere presence of these laws has caused activists to think twice, then these laws have already accomplished what we set out to do."

Food-disparagement statutes are a fairly new development. Thirteen states have passed such laws in the 1990s, and at least nine other states are reportedly considering similar legislation. Both proponents and nonproponents say the impetus for such legislation was the notorious 1989 *60 Minutes* telecast "'A' is for Apple." The program's message was that Alar, a chemical used to prevent pre-harvest rotting of apples, was the most potent carcinogen in the food supply. Most scientists subsequently concluded that demonstrating whether Alar contributed to cancer incidence in the *least* would be difficult.

To win a food-disparagement suit, a food producer must meet extremely high standards—even if the disparager has been recklessly apocalyptic.

In the panic that followed the CBS broadcast, apple sales plummeted overnight, even where farmers didn't use Alar. Apple growers sued CBS for damages but lost. Apple markets eventually recovered; but because apples, like beef, are perishable, the growers never recovered their losses. Some went out of business.

Egg farmers and emu ranchers (emus are flightless birds) have also filed claims under food-disparagement statutes. Ranchers in Texas filed a suit seeking damages in connection with a car commercial telecast in 1997. The comedic commercial featured a job-hunting Honda Civic driver named "Joe." One of his job interviews takes place at an emu ranch called "Fowl Technology," whose owner tells him: "Emus, Joe. It's the pork of the future."

Says one Texas emu producer: "Basically, Honda made people stop and look at emu meat, emu products, and the emu business as a joke." Unlike pork, he adds, emu meat is low in fat—and red. Honda officials say they meant no harm and describe the ad as tongue-in-cheek.

The other food-disparagement case involves Buckeye Egg Farm. Buckeye says an activist organization—the Ohio Public Interest Research

Group (OPIRG)—libeled its products by accusing the company of illegally repackaging old eggs and selling them as new. Buckeye Egg Farm is seeking unspecified damages. The company's president, Andy Hansen, reportedly told the Associated Press that Buckeye had followed federal guidelines and that these permit repackaging in certain circumstances. Hansen also noted that OPIRG had made its allegations public shortly before the Easter-egg season. "If there was no intent to disparage this product, why was it done at that time?" Hansen asked.

A biased broadcast

A long-term chill on the press from food-disparagement laws seems unlikely. Judge and jury in the Oprah case dismissed all charges. But to win a food-disparagement suit, a food producer must meet extremely high standards—even if the disparager has been recklessly apocalyptic.

Besides the Humane Society's Howard Lyman, guests on the "Dangerous Food" edition of Ms. Winfrey's talk show included Dr. Gary Weber—described as a spokesman for the National Cattlemen's Beef Association—and Dr. William Hueston of the U.S. Department of Agriculture. The program aired shortly after British officials had announced the linking of BSE to the deaths of ten people in their country. These ten people reportedly had eaten beef from cows infected with a certain feed contaminant. Dr. Hueston, whom Winfrey correctly described as a leading expert on "mad cow disease," told the studio audience that there was no evidence of the disease in the United States. But, because of editing, the broadcast did not include that pivotal statement. Neither did it include several other statements Hueston had made to the studio audience: that the risk of contracting the human equivalent of BSE was so small he would consume not only American beef but beef from Great Britain as well; that the U.S. Food and Drug Administration (FDA) had strictly regulated the feed in question; and that the cattle industry had voluntarily banned the feed and had requested an FDA ban.

Also omitted was former Surgeon General C. Everett Koop's public statement that consumers of American beef "should feel completely safe." Instead, the television audience heard former cattle rancher Lyman's claim that U.S. officials are "following exactly the same path that they followed in England." Some 100,000 cows that are fine at night, he said, are dead by morning—and most of them are ground up and fed to other cows. That unsubstantiated claim went largely unchallenged in the broadcast.

Winfrey made much of Lyman's transformation from cattleman to vegetarian Humane Society official, implying that he was a man of principle who had fled the cattle industry out of revulsion for its practices. Unknown to most of Winfrey's viewers, Lyman had sold his ranch to pay his debts; furthermore, he had weighed over 300 pounds when his physician advised him to change his eating habits and Lyman gave up eating meat.

Because of the degree of her show's influence—a book promoted thereon can consequently become a bestseller overnight—Ms. Winfrey owes it to her viewers and sponsors to deal accurately and comprehensively with any controversy her show covers. "Dangerous Food," to say the least, does not exemplify such an approach; and it is doubtful that existing food-disparagement laws will have much of an effect on talk shows.

Note

1. "BSE" stands for "bovine spongiform encephalopathy." The human equivalent of BSE is Creutzfeldt-Jacob disease (CJD). The type of CJD linked to BSE is called "new variant CJD," or "nvCJD."

14

Food-Disparagement Laws Could Threaten Food Safety

Ronald K.L. Collins

Ronald K.L. Collins is the director of the Foodspeak Project, a coalition organized by the Center for Science in the Public Interest to fight food-disparagement laws.

Food-disparagement laws pose a considerable threat to food safety by limiting the ability of activists and reporters to speak about potentially dangerous foods. These laws limit First Amendment rights while benefiting special business interests. The possibility of litigation means that food critics must either prepare for costly lawsuits when they choose to speak out or remain quiet about food safety threats. The scientific evidence standard in the laws—which requires that the food critics' claims be based on reliable scientific facts and data—further discourages open discussion because that evidence is frequently impossible to ascertain or is owned by the industry being criticized.

The costs of free speech are rising. Thanks to "veggie-libel" laws, speaking about the safety of the food supply may result in a long and expensive lawsuit, a huge damages award or criminal sanctions. Even if the speaker prevails in court, he or she must still bear the litigation costs.

A dozen states—Alabama, Arizona, Florida, Georgia, Idaho, Louisiana, Mississippi, North Dakota, Ohio, Oklahoma, South Dakota and Texas—have adopted food-disparagement statutes stipulating that food critics may be held civilly liable for claiming any "perishable food product or commodity" is unsafe for human consumption. A thirteenth state, Colorado, makes "libeling" food a crime. In California and Michigan, industry is pushing to get such laws on the books. Agribusiness also tried, unsuccessfully, to include a similar provision in the 1996 federal farm bill.

Many of the food-disparagement laws punish First Amendment–protected expression, establish a lower standard for civil liability, allow for punitive damages and attorneys fees for plaintiffs alone, and lend themselves to abusive litigation practices. Moreover, in most states that

Reprinted from Ronald K.L. Collins, "Veggie Libel: Agribusiness Seeks to Stifle Speech," *Multinational Monitor*, May 1998, reprinted with permission from the publisher.

have enacted these laws, food critics must demonstrate that their claims are grounded in reliable scientific facts and data. The net effect is to carve out a special law of defamation for the food industry—one benefiting special business interests.

It was the Texas food-disparagement law that gave rise to Texas ranchers' $10.3 million lawsuit against television talk-show host Oprah Winfrey and vegetarian activist Howard Lyman. The suit was filed after Lyman, on Winfrey's show, described factory farm practices—including the feeding of "rendered" cattle and other animals to cows—and Oprah responded that the revelation would stop her from eating another burger.

The development of veggie-libel laws

The campaign for food-disparagement laws grew out of the Alar controversy, nearly a decade ago. After a 1989 "60 Minutes" episode highlighted warnings by the Natural Resources Defense Council (NRDC) and actress Meryl Streep about the hazards of the plant growth regulator Alar (used on apples) and other pesticides, apple sales plummeted. Soon, Alar's maker, Uniroyal, removed it from the market.

The Alar case demonstrated how well-packaged information from public interest groups could mobilize consumer action.

Apple growers sued "60 Minutes" for the Alar report under traditional common law, and lost. A federal district court ruled that their claim of disparagement—the notion that the "60 Minutes" program injured the value of their property—required the growers to meet a high standard of proof, including a demonstration that the show's accusations were false. Concluding that the growers could not meet this high standard, the court dismissed their claim on summary judgment, before a jury was ever selected. The Court of Appeals for the Ninth Circuit affirmed the judgment and the U.S. Supreme Court declined to review the growers' appeal.

According to Steve Kopperud of the American Feed Industry Association, his group arranged with Dennis Johnson of the Washington, D.C., law firm of Olsson, Frank & Weeda to draft model food-disparagement legislation. Thereafter, the American Feed Industry Association and the American Farm Bureau Federation distributed the model legislation widely.

Under the common law, it is only possible to defame a person or corporation, not an object such as an apple. In order for an allegedly defamatory statement to give rise to a cause of action, the statement must be "of and concerning" a particular person or corporation. Absent that, a claim is constitutionally deficient. While standards vary by state and nature of a claim, in general, the common law and First Amendment require a plaintiff in a defamation or even disparagement case to prove an allegedly defamatory statement was untrue and that the speaker knew or should have known that it was untrue. First Amendment and state constitutional cases likewise suggest that the allegedly defamatory statements must be made with actual malice.

Food-disparagement laws, says Professor Rodney Smolla, a noted First Amendment authority at the William and Mary Law School, "dilute First Amendment standards and/or undermine the spirit of the principles underlying them. Some blur the line between expressions of opinion and false statements of fact. Others permit liability to be predicated on mere negligence, as opposed to knowing or reckless falsity. Still others appear to shift the burden of proof from the public figure plaintiff to the speaker."

Troubling laws

The veggie-libel laws' broad sweep and lax standards cast an intimidating shadow over citizen activists and independent-minded reporters and publishers, including book publishers.

In states with food-disparagement laws, comment on the health dangers of bacteria in meats and poultry, the threat of bacterial infection from raw oysters, sulfites in salads, nitrites in bacon and other processed foods, cholesterol in eggs, fat in milk and meat, food dyes, polluted fish, Alar-sprayed apples, pesticide-treated foods, non-pasteurized juices and contaminated grapes, among many other examples, could subject the speaker to a lawsuit.

Food-disparagement laws invite industry "libel" litigation against food critics—including critics such as the American Cancer Society, the American Heart Association and the Natural Resources Defense Council. In veggie-libel states, food critics must prepare themselves for costly litigation whenever they speak, regardless of the truth of their claims. The mere threat of such litigation could silence many would-be critics. The first Oprah case (there is now a second action in addition to the first case which is on appeal) cost nearly a million dollars to defend at the trial level alone. [The first case was still on appeal as of May 1999. No decision has been reached in the second suit.]

"The realistic objective of the frivolous 'veggie-libel' statutes and lawsuits is not money," says consumer advocate Ralph Nader. "It is to send a chilling message to millions of people that they better keep their opinions to themselves."

Individuals or media without the deep pockets to defend themselves are especially vulnerable to the chilling effect. "A consumer reporter for a small-market newspaper or TV station or a solo scientist putting out a food-safety newsletter is . . . very much at the mercy of agribiz," noted an editorial in the Press Journal of Vero Beach, Florida.

Food-disparagement laws are the "descendants of criminal sedition laws, which made it a crime to criticize public officials," says American Civil Liberties Union Executive Director Ira Glasser. "Today, such laws are used almost exclusively by the powerful to silence their critics."

In states with food-disparagement laws, comment on the health dangers of bacteria in meats and poultry . . . could subject the speaker to a lawsuit.

The scientific evidence standard of the veggie-libel laws further stands to discourage many critics, reporters and publishers from saying virtually anything about food absent current and documented scientific evidence, which quite often is impossible to determine or in the sole possession of the industry being criticized.

The chilling effect of food-disparagement laws may extend well beyond the immediate jurisdictions of the 13 states in which they exist. These laws have a national impact insofar as they subject internet users to runaway liability. For example, if a public interest group made statements on its web site about food and toxic waste, it might well be sued in any or all of the 13 states with these laws, even though the group may have no other contact with these states. Similarly, insofar as book publishers sell books in a national market, food-disparagement laws affect their decisions as to how robust an author's statements may be.

The cumulative effect of the veggie-libel laws will be most severe in deterring expression of new and controversial ideas about which the scientific community has not yet reached consensus. On this point Senator Patrick Leahy, D-Vermont, has noted that "one of the pioneers of the movement toward healthier eating—Adelle Davis—raised many food safety and health issues based on her own research. Her views were not accepted by the scientific community at the time. Now the weight of medical evidence—including former Surgeon General Koop's Report on Nutrition and Health—has vindicated her views."

The spread of food-disparagement laws may even have consequences outside of the particular matters to which the laws apply. A court victory for existing food laws could invite industry to push for all sorts of similar disparagement laws concerning everything from fast food to alcohol, and perhaps onto other consumer topics, such as auto safety. The net result: far less public talk about food and perhaps other consumer products by far fewer people.

Responding to the laws

The initial, ongoing and new lawsuits against Oprah Winfrey and Howard Lyman have brought attention to the threats posed by food-disparagement laws.

Winfrey and Lyman won their first case. Judge Mary Lou Robinson threw out the food-disparagement claim with a ringing, "It would be difficult to conceive of any topic of discussion that could be of greater concern and interest to all Americans than the safety of the food that they eat." And a jury rejected the cattle growers' common law claims.

But the case did not resolve whether veggie-libel laws violate the First Amendment. Unless that question is answered—and soon—others who lack the public profile or private resources of Winfrey could be dragged off to court for speaking out about food and food safety.

To "reclaim the First Amendment," the Center for Science in the Public Interest has organized a coalition of some 30 groups to oppose food-disparagement laws. The Foodspeak Coalition consists of a variety of public interest, health and nutrition, civil liberties, environmental and media groups, including Public Citizen, ACLU, United Farm Workers, Society of Professional Journalists, Publishers Marketing Association, Electronic Frontier Foundation and the Environmental Working Group. The Foodspeak campaign plans to contest food-disparagement laws on legislative, judicial and public information fronts.

The Coalition has plenty of work ahead of it, as evidenced by a lawsuit filed by Buckeye Egg Company of Ohio against the Ohio Public Interest Research Group (Ohio PIRG) and one of its employees, Amy Simpson.

The egg producer, which is represented by the giant law firm Jones, Day, Reavis & Pogue, alleged that the defendants, during the course of a press conference announcing a consumer action against Buckeye Egg, falsely and knowingly misrepresented that the company washed and repackaged old eggs for resale, and that such practices could be dangerous to public health.

The defendants countered that their charges were based on numerous interviews with and sworn statements by the company's own employees "who knew of the repackaging." NBC's "Dateline" confirmed the charge against Buckeye Egg of back-dating and reselling eggs.

Such facts notwithstanding, Simpson is being sued for saying: "[W]e have no idea how many, if any, consumers have been made ill by consuming these eggs." According to Buckeye's legal complaint, that statement was sufficiently "outrageous" to warrant a claim for compensatory and punitive damages plus attorneys fees (available under Ohio's law to plaintiffs only).

"The cost of speaking out has been high," says Amy Simpson. "All of us at Ohio PIRG have had to commit enormous amounts of time, energy, and resources to defend ourselves in this lawsuit. We have had to endure attacks by Buckeye's law firm, Jones, Day, one of the largest law firms in the world."

For that reason, Ralph Nader, Ira Glasser of the American Civil Liberties Union and Michael Jacobson, executive director of the Center for Science in the Public Interest, sent a letter on May 1, 1998 to Andy Hansen, president of Buckeye Egg Company, urging the company "to unconditionally drop this action immediately."

The letter states, "If you disagree with Ms. Simpson, debate her. If you feel strongly about the matter, use your resources to respond to her. But do not try to intimidate her by forcing her into impoverishment defending a lawsuit which you cannot ultimately win. This is not the American way."

Organizations to Contact

The editors have compiled the following list of organizations concerned with the issues debated in this book. The descriptions are derived from materials provided by the organizations. All have publications or information available for interested readers. The list was compiled on the date of publication of the present volume; the information provided here may change. Be aware that many organizations take several weeks or longer to respond to inquiries, so allow as much time as possible.

American Council on Science and Health (ACSH)
1995 Broadway, 2nd Fl., New York, NY 10023-5860
(212) 362-7044 • fax: (212) 362-4919
e-mail: acsh@acsh.org • website: http://www.acsh.org

ACSH provides consumers with scientific evaluations of food and the environment, pointing out both health hazards and benefits. It participates in a variety of government and media events, from congressional hearings to popular magazines. It publishes the bimonthly *News and Views*, as well as the booklets *Eating Safely: Avoiding Foodborne Illness*, *Biotechnology and Food*, and *Modernize the Food Safety Laws: Delete the Delaney Clause*.

Biotechnology Industry Organization (BIO)
1625 K St. NW, Suite 1100, Washington, DC 20006
(202) 857-0244 • fax: (202) 857-0237
e-mail: info@bio.org • website: http://www.bio.org

BIO represents biotechnology companies, academic institutions, and state biotechnology centers engaged in the development of products and services in the areas of biomedicine, agriculture, and environmental applications. It conducts workshops and produces educational activities aimed at increasing public understanding of biotechnology. Its publications include the bimonthly newsletter *BIO Bulletin*, the periodic *BIO News*, and the book *Biotech for All*.

Campaign for Food Safety (CFS)
860 Hwy. 61, Little Marais, MN 55614
(218) 226-4164 • fax: (218) 226-4157
e-mail: alliance@mr.net • website: http://www.purefood.org

The Campaign for Food Safety promotes the growth of organic and sustainable agriculture practices. CFS activist strategies include education, boycotts, grassroots lobbying, litigation, networking, direct action protests, and media events. It publishes the newsletter *Campaign for Food Safety News* as well as periodic *Action Alerts*.

Cato Institute
1000 Massachusetts Ave. NW, Washington, DC 20001-5403
(202) 842-0200 • fax: (202) 842-3490
e-mail: cato@cato.org • website: http://www.cato.org

The institute is a libertarian public policy research foundation dedicated to limiting the role of government and protecting individual liberties. It asserts that the concern over the possible health risks of pesticide use in agriculture is overstated. The institute publishes the quarterly *Cato Journal*, the bimonthly *Cato Policy Report*, and numerous books and commentaries.

Center for Science in the Public Interest (CSPI)
1875 Connecticut Ave. NW, Suite 300, Washington, DC 20009
 (202) 332-9110 • fax: (202) 265-4954
e-mail: cspi@cspinet.org • website: http://www.cspinet.org

The Center for Science in the Public Interest is a nonprofit education and advocacy organization committed to improving the safety and nutritional quality of the U.S. food supply. It publishes *Nutrition Action Healthletter*, the largest-circulation health newsletter in the country.

Environmental Protection Agency (EPA)
401 M St. SW, Washington, DC 20460
(202) 260-2090
e-mail: public-access@epamail.epa.gov • website: http://www.epa.gov

The EPA is a government agency that regulates pesticides under two major federal statutes. It establishes maximum legally permissible levels for pesticide residues in food, and it registers pesticides for use in the United States and prescribes labeling and other regulatory requirements to prevent unreasonable adverse effects on health or the environment. The agency publishes the bimonthly *EPA Journal* and numerous reports on environmental topics.

Food and Drug Administration (FDA)
5600 Fishers Lane, Rockville, MD 20857
(888) 463-6332
e-mail: webmail@oc.fda.gov • website: http://www.fda.gov

The FDA is a public health agency charged with protecting American consumers by enforcing the Federal Food, Drug, and Cosmetic Act and several related public health laws. To carry out this mandate of consumer protection, FDA has investigators and inspectors cover the country's almost ninety-five thousand FDA-regulated businesses. Its publications include government documents, reports, fact sheets, and press announcements.

Food First
398 60th St., Oakland, CA 94618
(510) 654-4400 • fax: (510) 654-4551
e-mail: foodfirst@foodfirst.org • website: http://www.foodfirst.org

Food First, founded by the author of *Diet for a Small Planet*, promotes sustainable agriculture. Its current projects include the Cuban Organic Agriculture Exchange Program and Californians for Pesticide Reform. It publishes the quarterly *Backgrounder* newsletter and several books.

Food Safety Consortium (FSC)
110 Agriculture Building, University of Arkansas, Fayetteville, AR 72701
(501) 575-5647 • fax: (501) 575-7531
e-mail: fsc@cavern.uark.edu • website: http://www.uark.edu/depts/fsc

Congress established the Food Safety Consortium, consisting of researchers from the University of Arkansas, Iowa State University, and Kansas State University, in 1988 through a special Cooperative State Research Service grant. It conducts extensive investigation into all areas of poultry, beef, and pork meat production. The consortium publishes the quarterly *FSC Newsletter*.

Friends of the Earth (FoE)
1025 Vermont Ave. NW, #300, Washington, DC 20005
(202) 783-7400 • fax: (202) 783-0444
e-mail: foe@foe.org • website: http://www.foe.org

Friends of the Earth monitors legislation and regulations that affect the environment. Its Safer Food, Safer Farms Campaign speaks out against what it perceives as the negative impact biotechnology can have on farming, food production, genetic resources, and the environment. It publishes the quarterly newsletter *Atmosphere* and the magazine *Friends of the Earth* ten times a year.

International Vegetarian Union (IVU)
PO Box 9710, Washington, DC 20016
(202) 362-8349
e-mail: vuna@ivu.org • website: http://www.ivu.org

The International Vegetarian Union is a nonprofit organization which advocates animal welfare, humanitarian, and health objectives. It publishes the annual *IVU News* and makes available on its website articles concerning food safety issues from affiliate vegetarian organizations.

Iowa State University—Bioethics Program
402 Catt Hall, Ames, IA 50011
(515) 294-5400
e-mail: comstock@iastate.edu • website: http://grad.admin.iastate.edu/bioethics/

The forum is an interdisciplinary group that focuses on the relationship between agriculture and bioethics. Among other issues, it explores the ethical dilemmas that arise when genetic engineering is applied to agriculture. The forum publishes the newsletter *Ag Bioethics Forum*.

National Cattlemen's Beef Association (NCBA)
5420 S. Quebec St., Greenwood Village, CO 80111-1905
(303) 694-0305 • fax: (303) 694-2851
e-mail: cattle@beef.org • website: http://www.beef.org

National Cattlemen's Beef Association is the marketing organization and trade association for America's 1 million cattle farmers and ranchers. Its Food Safety library publishes the quarterly *Food and Nutrition* newsletter, the fact sheet "Progress in Food Safety: Toward a Safer Beef Supply," and the booklet *Plating It Safe*.

National Food Safety Database
University of Florida
3082 McCarty Hall B, PO Box 110287, Gainesville, FL 32611
(352) 846-2270 • fax: (352) 846-1102
e-mail: alla@gnv.ifas.ufl.edu • website: http://www.foodsafety.org

The National Food Safety Database project is an organization funded primarily by the USDA in order to develop an efficient management system of U.S. food safety databases. Numerous food safety fact sheets, including "Preventing Foodborne Illnesses," "Myths About Food Safety," and "Botulism—It Only Takes a Taste," are available on its website.

U.S. Department of Agriculture (USDA)
Food Safety and Inspection Service (FSIS)
1400 Independence Ave. SW, Room 2932-S, Washington, DC 20250-3700
(202) 720-7943 • fax: (202) 720-1843
e-mail: fsiswebmaster@usda.gov • website: http://www.fsis.usda.gov

The Food Safety and Inspection Service is the public health agency of the USDA responsible for ensuring that the nation's commercial supply of meat, poultry, and egg products is safe, wholesome, and correctly labeled and packaged. It publishes fact sheets, reports, articles, and brochures on food safety topics.

Bibliography

Books

Dennis T. Avery — *Saving the Planet with Pesticides and Plastic: The Environmental Triumph of High-Yield Farming.* Indianapolis, IN: Hudson Institute, 1995.

James T. Bennett and Thomas J. DiLorenzo — *The Food and Drink Police: America's Nannies, Busybodies, and Petty Tyrants.* New Brunswick, NJ: Transaction, 1996.

Kristin Dawkins — *Gene Wars: The Politics of Biotechnology.* New York: Seven Stories Press, 1997.

Gail A. Eisnitz — *Slaughterhouse: The Shocking Story of Greed, Neglect, and Inhumane Treatment Inside the U.S. Meat Industry.* Amherst, NY: Prometheus Books, 1997.

Michael W. Fox — *Beyond Evolution: The Genetically Altered Future of Plants, Animals, the Earth—Humans.* New York: Lyons Press, 1999.

Nicols Fox — *Spoiled: The Dangerous Truth About a Food Chain Gone Haywire.* New York: BasicBooks, 1997.

Brewster Kneen — *Farmageddon: Food and the Culture of Biotechnology.* Gabriola Island, British Columbia, Canada: New Society, 1999.

Sheldon Krimsky — *Agricultural Biotechnology and the Environment: Science, Policy, and Social Issues.* Urbana: University of Illinois Press, 1996.

Marc Lappôe and Britt Bailey — *Against the Grain: Biotechnology and the Corporate Takeover of Your Food.* Monroe, ME: Common Courage Press, 1998.

Sara L. Latta — *Food Poisoning and Foodborne Diseases.* Springfield, NJ: Enslow, 1999.

Robin Mather — *A Garden of Unearthly Delights: Bioengineering and the Future of Food.* New York: Penguin Books, 1995.

Ben Mepham, ed. — *Food Ethics.* London: Routledge, 1996.

Stephen Nottingham — *Eat Your Genes: How Genetically Modified Food Is Entering Our Diet.* New York: St. Martin's Press, 1998.

Sheldon Rampton and John Stauber — *Mad Cow U.S.A.: Could the Nightmare Happen Here?* Monroe, ME: Common Courage Press, 1997.

Richard Rhodes — *Deadly Feasts: Tracking the Secrets of a Terrifying New Plague.* New York: Simon & Schuster, 1997.

Rosalind M. Ridley — *Fatal Protein: The Story of CJD, BSE, and Other Prion Diseases.* New York: Oxford University Press, 1998.

Elizabeth Scott and Paul Sockett — *How to Prevent Food Poisoning: A Practical Guide to Safe Cooking, Eating, and Food Handling*. New York: John Wiley & Sons, 1998.

George J. Seperich — *Food Science and Safety*. Danville, IL: Interstate Publishers, 1998.

Paul B. Thompson — *Food Biotechnology in Ethical Perspective*. New York: Blackie Academic & Professional, 1997.

Kerry S. Walters and Lisa Portmess, eds. — *Ethical Vegetarianism: From Pythagoras to Peter Singer*. Albany: State University of New York Press, 1999.

Periodicals

Dennis Avery — "Feeding the World with Biotech Crops," *World & I*, May 1998. Available from 3600 New York Ave. NE, Washington, DC 20002.

James T. Bennett and Thomas J. DiLorenzo — "Regulatory Poison," *Freeman*, February 1998. Available from the Foundation for Economic Education, Irvington-on-Hudson, NY 10533.

Joel Bleifuss — "What's in the Beef?" *In These Times*, April 15–28, 1996.

Jane E. Brody — "Adding Cumin to the Curry: A Matter of Life and Death," *New York Times*, March 3, 1998.

Kenny Bruno — "Say It Ain't Soy, Monsanto," *Multinational Monitor*, January/February 1997.

Daniel M. Byrd — "Goodbye Pesticides?" *Regulation*, Fall 1997. Available from 1000 Massachusetts Ave. NW, Washington, DC 20001. Available online at http://www.cato.org.

Jennifer Ferrara — "The Great Pesticide Compromise: How Many Deaths for a Dollar?" *Everyone's Backyard*, Fall 1996.

Michael Fumento — "Fear of Fruit," *Wall Street Journal*, February 26, 1999.

Bill Grierson — "Food Safety Through the Ages," *Priorities*, vol. 9, no. 3, 1997. Available from 1995 Broadway, 2nd Floor, New York, NY 10023-5860. Available online at http://www.acsh.org.

Gayle M.B. Hanson — "Is Something Rotten in the U.S. Meat Market?" *Insight*, December 30, 1996. Available from 3600 New York Ave. NE, Washington, DC 20002.

Thom Hartmann — "No Place to Escape," *Tikkun*, May/June 1999.

Issues and Controversies On File — "Food Safety," February 23, 1996. Available from Facts On File News Service, 11 Penn Plaza, New York, NY 10001-2006.

Kathy Koch — "Food Safety Battle: Organic vs. Biotech," *CQ Researcher*, September 4, 1998. Available from 1414 22nd St. NW, Washington, DC 20037.

Gina Kolata with Christopher Drew — "Long Quest for Safer Food Revisits Radiation Method," *New York Times*, December 4, 1997.

JoAnn Lum	"Sweatshops Are Us," *Dollars & Sense*, September 19, 1997.
Asoka Mendis and Caroline Van Bers	"Bitter Fruit," *Alternatives Journal*, Winter 1999.
Tom Morganthau	"E. Coli Alert," *Newsweek*, September 1, 1997.
Multinational Monitor	"Campaigning for Food Safety: An Interview with Ronnie Cummins," December 1998.
Kieran Mulvaney	"Mad Cows and the Colonies," *E Magazine*, July/August 1996.
Robert Pear	"Tougher Labeling for Organic Food," *New York Times*, May 9, 1998.
Amy Poe	"Media Zapped," *Extra!* March/April 1998.
Ellen Ruppel Shell	"Could Mad-Cow Disease Happen Here?" *Atlantic Monthly*, September 1998.
Amanda Spake	"O Is for Outbreak," *U.S. News & World Report*, November 24, 1997.
Donovan Webster	"The Stink About Pork," *George*, April 1999. Available from 30 Montgomery St., Jersey City, NJ 07032.

Index